Who Am I?

The Self Empowerment Journey (SEJ) Handbook

Jacqueline Mary Phillips

Dedication

I ask all those who have purchased this book to dedicate it to someone who is suffering. My reason for this? Everyone suffers (to a lesser or greater degree) at some point in their life. No one should be left to suffer without the necessary tools within which to empower themselves.

Thank you x

Who Am I?

Acknowledgments

To Sadhguru without whom this book would not have been possible. Deepest Gratitude.
https://isha.sadhguru.org/uk/en

To my darling husband, you taught me more than you will ever know. Thank you. x

To my daughters, you made my life into an offering, a phenomenal way to dissolve myself. Thank you. x

To Dr. Mariko Howard-Kishi for writing the back cover and being instrumental to our work in education, and an advocate of the SEJ. Thank you. x

To Carol Blakemore, our longest standing volunteer at the SEJ Foundation, thank you for everything!

To Elliot Hughes, thank you for writing the Introduction and bringing new life and energy into the business, enabling more people to access the SEJ Process.

It is due to all of you this book is here today.

THANK YOU x

Who Am I?

Contents

	Introduction	9
1	The past	13
2	The beginning of the end suffering and freedom	15
3	I realised my mind, body and emotions worked as one	19
4	I was the one I had always been looking for	21
5	What is Truth?	30
6	Awareness crept in	32
7	Therapy is missing the Truth	36
8	Everything changed	39
9	Why do we suffer?	41
10	It's a bad habit	43
11	The mind can never see reality	44
12	Truth is who you are	48
13	From unconscious to conscious living	51

14	Truth or intuition	56
15	Thoughts have no power	58
16	You cannot control your thoughts	61
17	Most people believe they are their thoughts	63
18	You are a storyteller	65
19	Positive thinking and willpower do not work	67
20	The SEJ Process	69
21	How to complete the SEJ Worksheet	72
22	SEJ worksheet examples	87
23	Einstein and the SEJ	115
24	What thoughts should I question?	120
25	Your SELF Empowerment Journey	125
26	The SEJ and the law of attraction	128
27	Try it for yourself	131
28	Frequently Asked Questions	133
29	Conclusion	142
	Appendix	143
	About the Author	156

Introduction

Mary through this book will begin sharing with you a process that helps us all find freedom from fearful thoughts and painful emotions.

A process that works 100% of the time if you use it and follow through on the instructions.

A process that is simple to learn and simple to use.

A process that will help YOU find freedom from those thoughts that we believe to be true. That at best can prevent us from living a life of passion and joy, and at worst can lead to mental health issues including depression.

A process that has been used with countless individuals from all walks of life, ages, and backgrounds for over 24 years.

I first became aware of Mary and the process that she is going to share with you all in this wonderful book, when I was living a pretty normal, and what I thought at the time was a successful and fulfilling life.

I turned up at one of Mary's classes as one of those slightly stressed corporate types looking for a bit of relaxation through meditation or whatever process she would share with me. What happened after that completely changed 'my world', but more importantly how I viewed 'my world'.

Before I met Mary and she shared the process with me, the same process that she is sharing with you in this book, I thought my life was okay. All I was looking for was a few easy techniques to help me relax and deal with the minor stresses that we all face in our lives; work, money, and such like.

I began using the process and many areas of my life improved, and then I went off on my merry way thinking "that was brilliant, but I don't need any help anymore."

My life improved, I had a wonderful corporate job that brought me more money than I'd ever earned before, relationships, I had lots of friends and a nice house in the countryside.

It was at this point that something quite profound happened. I had everything I wanted, and my life was "OK," but I found myself becoming increasingly stressed, and unhappy. I was sliding into (although I did not realise it at the time) a state of depression.

"How could this be? I have everything that I wanted."

It was at this moment in my life that I remembered the process that Mary shared with me. Needless to say, I began to re-apply the process to my life, and changes happened immediately. No longer was I living a life of sadness, doubt, fear, and depression.

My life has changed beyond my wildest dreams. I now live a life of joy and passion to such an extent that I have the honour and pleasure to not only be writing the Introduction to this book, but to now be part of the team, with Mary that is sharing this process with the world.

Live in joy! Elliot

"Self Empowerment is the realisation of the True Self beyond the mind. This realisation puts you in touch with a Self that is free of limitations, free of fearful thoughts and painful emotions, free to respond to life rather than react, free to reach your full potential.

The Self Empowerment Journey - SEJ is a process that takes you to this realisation."

Jacqueline Mary Phillips

Chapter One

The past

The past undoubtedly affects our present and future. It is therefore important I establish a foundation for this book, and the SEJ Process, by presenting to you a brief outline of my childhood experiences. Sharing how they typically led me to experience depression and in turn the Self Empowerment Journey (SEJ) process.

I had suffered with depression off and on since the age of fourteen, at least that was the age I gained an understanding of the meaning of depression. Although looking back I remember feeling 'depressed' from quite an early age, even as young as seven.

I never really felt as if I fitted in, not even with my own family. Most days I would wake up with an overwhelming sense of nervous dread and heaviness, not wanting to do anything. I would typically spend my childhood days keenly observing life as it unfolded around me, feeling an overriding sense of complete disconnection from my family.

As a young child I was sexually abused, but it was really the mental and emotional abuse that affected me the most. Naturally, many years later the professionals attributed the depression to these childhood traumas.

I was officially diagnosed with depression in my early twenties, although the first time I visited the doctor was at the age of seventeen. Throughout my twenties I suffered three severe bouts of depression and by the time I was in my late twenties I was hospitalised in a psychiatric hospital, and not for the first time. During this final stay in hospital I attempted suicide. I was absolutely clear in my mind I no longer wanted to live. This hospitalisation lasted about 2 years with some home leave.

Chapter Two

The beginning of the end - Suffering and Freedom

It was during this challenging time that I experienced 'Truth', there really is no other way of correctly describing it. Put differently, I saw that everything I was thinking and believing was an absolute lie.

I could instantly see my thoughts were repetitive in nature and not based on reality. I sincerely believed the thoughts I was experiencing were mine, then one day they were not 'MY' thoughts anymore, they were just thoughts. The separation between 'MY' thoughts and **'a thought'** was the essential difference between suffering and freedom.

Suffering was a daily experience during my time in the psychiatric hospital. In fact, I had pretty much suffered my whole life, until this pivotal moment.

I was sitting comfortably in my psychiatrist's consulting room, she was the most remarkable woman, filled with love and compassion. I genuinely did like her a lot and, I knew she wanted to do her absolute best for me.

On this particular day, she reluctantly informed me, that because of my personal history of trauma, depression, and my family history, (my dad had suffered terribly with mental health issues for most of his adult life). I would most likely suffer with depression for the rest of my life. Periodically experiencing recurring bouts of depression as had been my experience thus far. The best that could be done for me was to learn and adopt techniques to manage my depression. Hearing this just broke me, quite literally broke me in two, I felt like two different people. Allow me to explain.

Going back a couple of weeks or so before my appointment with my psychiatrist, I had found all I could think about was desperately wanting to die; I'd had enough, life was a personal hell and I saw no reason to carry on. My dominant thought was 'I don't want to live.' It was a constant thought going round and round in my head, the more I tried not thinking that way the more I did. The thought was true, for me it was true, so why not think that way, I wanted out.

When my psychiatrist informed me, I would most likely suffer depressive episodes for the rest of my life this dominant thought changed, and with just two inspired words added onto the initial thought it became 'I don't want to live LIKE THIS!' I didn't know where the thought came from, it just seemed to rise from within me, gently and yet powerfully. It felt so freeing, I would even say I felt excited by the new inspired thought.

I instantly felt like two different people, one was thinking 'I don't want to live' and another thinking 'I don't want to live *like this.*' There was this overwhelming feeling of freedom in the awareness that I in fact didn't want to die. **The Truth** was that I didn't want to live *like this.*

Once I had realised deeply the liberating truth I didn't want to live *'like this'* the realisations kept coming, this truth invariably meant that not only did I want to live, but there must moreover be another way of living, a better way of living. *'Like this'* undoubtedly meant there must be another way. Does this seem obvious? Because it did to me too, the moment I discovered this as a limitless possibility, that there was another way to live. When I believed the thought, 'I don't want to live' it hadn't ever occurred to me that my life could be different, all I could envisage was the helpless misery that was depression, therefore that was all I could experience.

The next realisation was the positive change in my emotion. I suddenly didn't feel depressed, I experienced a range of emotions from anger to excitement. It felt amazing, this feeling of anger after feeling so severely depressed felt liberating. I was feeling something, instead of the awful numb or desperate feelings. Again, an enormous sense of freedom, freedom from the horrific emotional prison of debilitating depression.

I felt angry towards my psychiatrist, not her personally but about what she had said. I remember thinking 'who does she think she is telling me what my life will be like, she doesn't know me.' Again, my awareness expanded, and I suddenly saw that this loving and compassionate woman, well-educated with many years' experience in her field, had no awareness of what I now knew! I saw clearly, she only recognised what she had been taught, and what she had been typically taught was severely limited in terms of perception and awareness. I know again this seems obvious, of course; she would only know what she had been taught. However, what I was witnessing was just how limiting that is, and that there were absolute truths far beyond that which she could perceive.

To perceive truth, I realised one must go beyond that which they have learnt. What the mind offers is always limited. That which is beyond mind, Truth, is limitless and will therefore enable a person to see beyond their limitations, experience life enhancing emotions and take new inspired action.

Now at this point I must add that I am not devaluing the work of my psychiatrist, or indeed any health care professional, who supported me whilst in their care. I shall be eternally grateful for their love. However, what I was able to see from an elevated state of consciousness, was more than they could see, more than they knew, more than what is written in any medical journal, more than they had been taught, so much more.

My awareness kept expanding over the days and weeks to come, indeed it has never stopped.

Chapter Three

I realised my mind, body and emotions worked as one

My awareness continued expanding experientially; I could now see how my unconscious thoughts adversely affected my emotional state. Consequently, the power and ultimate truth of the thought 'I don't want to live like this' changed my emotions. I felt excited, even enthusiastic. This, in turn, invariably changed my physical; I was sitting upright, I felt strong in my body, not something I had experienced in a long time. Next there was physical action; I became fascinated in what the truth 'like this' meant and promptly took inspired action to explore this truth. The action I was inspired to take again came from Truth, not from me.

I realised whatever thought I gave my attention to, trigger my emotions, physical sensations, and caused me to act in a certain way. Unconscious thoughts inevitably determined how I experienced myself and life. The crippling fearful emotions I had been experiencing were triggered by my thoughts. The limiting and often debilitating actions I took, were triggered by my thoughts.

The pain and sensations in my body were triggered by my thoughts. But only when I believed the thoughts, when I questioned them, truthful thoughts arose from within me. It was a move from unconscious to conscious living.

Chapter Four

I was the one I had always been looking for

With the truth 'I don't want to live like this' I instantly felt like I had a purpose. I wanted to prove my psychiatrist wrong, not so I could be right, but because I absolutely could not accept her truth. Somehow, I just knew there was another way.

This was yet another powerful realisation; I could see how people projected onto others their beliefs (what they genuinely believed to be true). How easily unconscious people typically took on the unconscious beliefs of others, seldom questioning, especially when given by a person of authority, educated in their field. Which, of course is exactly what I had done, until this key moment.

Who was I to question someone like my psychiatrist? After all she was educated, trained to do this work, and more intelligent than I. What a completely disempowering belief this was. If I were to put that belief through the SEJ now, I would likely come out with, 'who am I not to question someone like you,' and of course this is exactly what I did.

I knew my psychiatrist genuinely felt she was doing the 'right' thing by sharing her professional opinion with me, that I should accept and come to terms with depression, merely learn to live with it as I would likely suffer with depressive episodes throughout my life. But I could not accept this because I absolutely knew it was untrue. Back then I did not understand how I knew, but there was no questioning what I was experiencing, I just knew she was wrong. I was to prove to myself that I did not have to suffer with depression for the rest of my life. That the experts were wrong, not through any fault of their own, simply wrong through lack of awareness.

I had never truly been happy or joyful, yes there were moments, but my default was always a depressed state. As I continued to awaken to truth, I was aware of this depressed mood, but now there was also this Truth, a shift in awareness. Once more, it was like living as two people. I did not understand what or who these two people were, now I refer to them as the True and false selves. I was inspired from this True Self to speak to my psychotherapist, as my intention was to invite her to share with me a possible reason to live, an explanation to living 'like this'.

Now my psychotherapist was another remarkable woman, I would go as far as to say I idolised her, there was this deep connection between us. She typically saw me twice weekly, and I existed purely to see her. She had become my sole reason for living. I hated every moment in-between the sessions, my life had become one of just waiting to see her, I felt so strongly she was going to 'fix' me. One day she would sort me out, and everything would be OK.

After my realisation I went to my psychotherapist and informed her that if she could not give me a reason to live, I was prepared to die. I was asking her in the fervent hope that she would enlighten me as to what 'I don't want to live *like this'* meant, to give me the answer as to what other way there was of living. I was prepared to die and meant it. Although I did not feel she believed me. You see I was unafraid to die; my biggest fear was living. I needed to understand what was meant by 'to live like this' otherwise there was no reason to continue, death would inevitably deliver to me my answer.

She could not answer my burning question. She could not provide me with a valid reason to live. All the possible reasons for living felt ridiculous to me, reasons such as my husband loves me, I have an excellent job to go back to. None of this carried any weight; it felt as if nothing was worth living for.

I was completely shocked that she could not give me a valid reason to live. I had felt very strongly that if I were to ask her the question, that she knowingly would provide me with an answer. Yet, where the answer came from was even more shocking.

The answer came from within me.

I sat in the consulting room, experiencing immense disappointment in my psychotherapist. I had invested all my love, energy, and attention in her. I genuinely believed she was going to 'fix' me, and yet she could not answer my question. I felt devastated at the realisation that no-one could fix me. If she could not fix me then no one could. Throughout this experience I still felt like two people sharing one body. The one part of me, felt desperate with fearful thoughts such as 'what am I going to do now' realising that death was now my sole option. The other part of me, was simply observing what was happening.

I earnestly urged her again to provide me with a reason not to kill myself. It was the final attempt from the part of me that desperately needed her to be my saviour. To this negative and lost part of me, (false self) without her, there was no hope, because I couldn't help myself, or so I believed. The other part of me (True Self) was again simply observing what was unfolding.

What occurred next really is beyond remarkable and words will never be enough to express the profoundness of the experience.

Whilst sitting in my psychotherapist's consulting room, I experienced what I can only now describe as a powerful and profound shift in awareness and perception. In that extraordinary moment, my consciousness shifted to another time and space. What I experienced was beyond anything my rational mind could fathom and yet again there was this conscious awareness. A complete knowing that everything I was experiencing was absolute Truth.

Before I continue, I want to share with you a little of my background. I was raised as an atheist; I barely knew anything of religion or spirituality. I had traditionally worked in commerce, and had a very analytical mind, 'prove it' was my personal philosophy in life. Indeed, it still is. I constantly say to anyone practicing the SEJ process 'don't believe me, in fact I don't wish you to believe me, I genuinely want you to use the SEJ and prove it to yourself.'

To continue, I was aware my physical body was in the consulting room, but 'I' was not. I was in what I can only now describe as another time and dimension. One might reasonably describe it as a past life.

Somehow, I saw myself with a rope round my neck hanging from a tree; I had committed suicide. I was a young woman who had committed suicide because her abusive uncle (my father in my present life), had just murdered the baby she had given birth to and conceived by him.

There was no money to feed any more children, so he ruthlessly murdered the baby. My sister (my psychotherapist in this life) was at the foot of the tree naturally upset and angry saying 'why did you do it'? 'Why didn't you come to me'? I knew she genuinely felt she had failed me; I was experiencing her distressing emotions and thoughts as if they were my own.

As my sister in the past life, and now my psychotherapist in my current life, she had made a vow (although she did not consciously do it) through the words she had spoken. The vow would ensure she supported me in my next life. She would be there for me when I needed her, I absolutely knew we were inextricably bound to each other.

Even though in the past life I had committed suicide, I was still aware of all that was happening. I was even aware I had died and yet somehow was still alive, only the physical form had died. I could hear everything my sister was saying and felt her unbearable pain and anguish. As I continued to observe and experience her pain and suffering, I was left feeling guilty for abandoning her and regret at having taken my own life.

My sister then disappeared. I found myself in what I can only describe as limbo. I literally felt stuck, an eternal sense of floating aimlessly, with overwhelming feelings of guilt and regret. My body was gone, but I was not.

As I observed myself in the limbo state, I knew that even this was self-created. I had kept myself in limbo because of my fearful thoughts, I was torturing myself, there was no God doing anything to me. In an instant I was free from the eternal suffering of my own 'self'. An unspeakable suffering that had led me to this pivotal point in my current life.

My eyes were closed and when I opened them, I genuinely felt I had been gone a long time, but my Psychotherapist said nothing had happened. I carefully explained everything; I had seen she was my sister, and I had my much-needed answer. I kept hearing the words in my mind 'you'll have to do it all again.'

It was absolutely clear to me, as the words rang true 'you'll have to do it all again.' I absolutely knew if I committed suicide the cycle of depression and suicide would repeat itself. I would reincarnate to do it all again until I was free, and that only I could free myself. No one could 'fix' me. I was trapped in a birth, death, re-birth cycle. The only one that could release me was me. I was the one I had always been looking for.

I know it seems incredible, and you may well have some ideas about or even read of past and future lives. Whether you believe in past lives and reincarnation or not, I did not have any specific reference to such things at that point in my life. It was only much later that I could put words to my experience.

Through this extraordinary experience I had been instantly given all the information I needed. I understood the birth, death re-birth cycle. How we reincarnate with the same people, my sister (psychotherapist) my uncle (father). How we all repeat patterns of behaviour and are reborn to try and break the cycle. I not only understood the birth, death, re-birth cycle deeply, more importantly I realised what need to be done to break the cycle of endless suffering.

What I undoubtedly had was the answer to my unanswered question. I would have to come back and do it all again if I took my own life, I would reincarnate. There would be another life typically repeating the same mistakes and patterns of behaviour until I was free of them. I also knew there was no God punishing me, that I was at the centre of my own experience. The only person keeping me trapped in this karmic cycle, was me, so I was the only person that could free me. I was trapped by my own thoughts about myself, others, and life.

I looked knowingly at my psychotherapist; the 'false self' still somewhat disappointed that she was not the one with my answers. The True Self simply in a place of knowing. I was truly clear that my unanswered question had been unequivocally answered. If I took my own life, I would have to reincarnate and do it all again.

When I left the consulting room and I allowed myself space to re-visit what had happened; I knew that no-one could ever have my answers. That everyone is both the question and the answer. The one person you have always been looking for is inside of you, hidden beneath the karmic structures held in place by thoughts believed.

As you read this, you might feel hugely empowered by this statement, that you do not need anyone to fix you, or you might initially feel as I did, somewhat disconcerted, even upset as so much of yours (and my) life had been spent in the fruitless search of the one (person or treatment) that was ultimately going to fix you.

For some people, whose suffering is not so bad that they need fixing, instead go in search of love. Seeking the one that will complete them. It is the same empty search. You are the one you have always been looking for, you are the love of your life.

Chapter Five

What is Truth?

The seamless experience in my psychotherapist's room marked the beginning of my SELF empowerment journey. Everything identified as Truth through my experiences was later formulated into the SEJ process for everyone to use.

The Truth and freedom from suffering can be realised through using the process as this conscious process came from Truth, not from my own thinking. It was not something I created, but rather something that was created through me.

We must inevitably go beyond our own thinking and access Truth if we are ever going to stop identifying with our thoughts. And repeating patterns of thought and behaviour that cause us to suffer.

What is Truth? Truth is what rises from within a person beyond mind. It can appear as a thought; however, it is not the thought of the 'false' self. The Truth rises from within and uses the mind, body, and emotions as tools within which to communicate and express the Self through. It does not identify with anything or anyone and yet is everything and everyone.

I realised the profound truth that ended my suffering in the words 'I don't want to live **like this,**' when for so long I had incorrectly believed the thought 'I don't want to live.' It absolutely is that simple.

I was trapped in well-established patterns of thought, which caused me to experience depressing emotions and fearful bodily sensations. These led me to repeat a destructive behaviour, in this instance suicide. I invariably saw I could only be free from this destructive and limiting cycle once Truth was realised.

Chapter Six

Awareness crept in

Through this journey the depression stayed with me for a short while yet was experienced in an unusual way. I was acutely aware that as the false self, the old version of me that I was still at times identified with, felt some form of depression. I smoked a lot, and I could still be negative in my thoughts and emotions, but something else had also crept in – 'awareness'. I was still experiencing life as two people. The new me (True Self) observed life and myself from a different perspective. As the True Self it was as if I was separate somehow from my mind, body, and emotions.

I could see that when I believed a thought it triggered within me an emotional and physical reaction. As most of my thoughts had been negative so were my emotions, physical sensations, and actions.

I recall quite clearly one instance. I had just finished a very disappointing session with my psychotherapist, the sessions were not the same after my 'awakening'. I felt my psychotherapist had nothing to offer me anymore in terms of expertise, I remember just sitting with her, almost playing along so as not to disappoint her. I left her consulting room and went back to my own room in the hospital, I just sat on the floor crying. I recall crying very loudly and before long several friends (fellow patients) overheard me and came to cheer me up. It was as if the false part of me wanted to still be acknowledged, I was witnessing it 'acting out' to get attention.

I remember thinking (as my True Self) that I feel OK, and there really was nothing to cry about, as nothing was happening. I didn't say anything to my friends as they gathered round me, typically assuming I was troubled because of my psychotherapy session. I was observing myself crying just as I observed myself playing along with my psychotherapist. I cried for what seemed like an incredibly long time. Then suddenly the uncontrollable crying promptly stopped, next I stood up thanked everyone and we dutifully went for our evening meal.

Have you ever done that, observed yourself reacting in a certain way knowing that you could stop if you truly wanted to? Did you ever wonder who was the one reacting, and who was the one observing? This is the beginning of disidentifying with your past, who you believe you are (false self).

I knew nothing was ever going to be the same again. I was not the fearful person I once was, I was almost playacting, intentionally trying to be the old version of me, the person I identified with. I was gradually being introduced to who I really was, the one that just observed my 'playacting', my

True Self.

As the days and weeks went on, I seldom listened to my thoughts anymore. Instead, I seemed to have this internal knowing that would at times found a voice. I became increasingly silent both internally and externally. I simply had nothing to say most of the time, realising that most of what I had said previously was pointless and irrelevant.

There was one time when a young woman was brought into the hospital. She had been there a few days, but no one was allowed to speak with her or go into her room. There were private security guards by her door, which was most unusual.

One day she came into the lounge. She looked depressed, and it was clear she had, like many of us been self-harming. I turned towards her and asked if she was from aristocracy. At which point everyone looked at her and me. She naturally inquired as to how I knew, I could only tell her that I didn't know how I knew, I just did. She promptly took me aside and whispered anxiously in my ear, informing me that no one must know about her because of who she was related to.

As time went on, I became more aware of what to say and what not to say, even how to say it and when to say it. Words (Truths) stopped just falling out of my mouth, which is how it appeared to me. I began to see that Truth was not always welcome when a person was unconscious. Indeed, for many the false self becomes more pronounced when faced with Truth, feeling the need to justify, defend or attack for fear of its own demise.

As time passed, I became more conscious, and my awareness continued to grow. I found that other patients were naturally drawn to me, asking me questions, wanting answers, and not just the patients but the staff too. One student nurse was extremely interested in the inspired insights I was sharing and asked if he could speak with me in relation to his studies as a psychiatric nurse. Something inside of him knew there was more to learn than what he was being taught.

My relationship with my psychotherapist was changing too. I was becoming more empowered and driven by truth, but there were still times when the old part of me wanted everything to stay as they used to be. I knew things could never be the same. My relationships with everyone were changing.

Chapter Seven

Therapy is missing the Truth

During one memorable session with my psychotherapist, I suddenly saw in my mind's eye her son, whom I had never met. He was walking on a zebra crossing to get to an off-licence. He wanted to buy some alcohol as some of his friends were coming round to the house to watch a football match. I looked at my psychotherapist and apologised for what I was about to say but felt so strongly she must know.

Truth spoke through me from a dimension far beyond the capabilities of mind, this was happening increasingly. The stiller my mind became the more enhanced my abilities to see beyond this reality. The ability to see possible alternate realities, past and future and that which was vibrating at levels beyond those the physical eye could see were becoming more accessible to me.

I shared with my psychotherapist that her son would leave the house, cross a zebra crossing and get knocked down by a car. Her face went white, she apologised and excused herself to phone home, I gently urged her to do so.

On her return she willingly told me her son was indeed just putting his coat on to go to the off-licence. The reason she listened to me, was that I had told her he needed to cross a zebra crossing to get to the off-licence. This was something I could not possibly know. He had invited friends round to watch a football match; after the phone call he stayed home.

My psychotherapist was visibly shaken and apologetic, the professional boundaries of our relationship was now blurred. I would never take anything away from the heartfelt love and compassion shown to me by my psychotherapist. Yet the therapeutic process I could see, was not only outdated but disempowering. The only thing it kept alive was my 'false self'.

As we were working towards ending our sessions together during one of the last sessions, she explained to me that I could now go out in the world and live my life, and that I did not need to forgive my father and mother, that forgiveness was unnecessary for me to move on.

I politely explained to her that forgiveness was absolutely necessary and indeed I had already forgiven them. I could see why my dad had abused me, how he too had been abused mentally and physically and how these cycles continue until someone stops them.

Genuine forgiveness happens naturally when we question our unforgiving thoughts, thoughts which keep the destructive cycle and bonds alive. I knew I was the one to break the cycle, and if I possessed anything less than love in my heart, by love I mean clarity of sight, conscious awareness, then there would be no end for him or me.

It was at this key point I truly recognised that the 'Truth' was missing in all the different therapeutic processes that I had tried. And whilst it is missing, the best that therapy can offer is to provide a sticking plaster. This, of course, is fine if you just want to protect the wound. But if you want to live fully, live an empowered life without the limitations unconsciously placed upon you by those around you and passed on from generation to generation. Maybe even know the Truth of who you are and end the birth, death re-birth cycle, then therapy cannot help.

I willingly stayed in therapy for a brief time after my awakening to Truth, in part to honour the therapeutic process, to see how it would end. And because of everything that the dedicated professionals had lovingly done for me. I did not feel any need to end the relationships, as again because of this inner knowing of Truth I absolutely knew they would come to a natural end, and they did.

It was time to leave and live as my True SELF. I knew everything in my life was about to change forever.

Chapter Eight

Everything changed

After therapy I left my friends, my husband, my home and moved to a different area. All this happened without any decision making, everything connected to the false self (or rather the false self's desires) just naturally fell away from me. I was a different person, driven by Truth and as such life was taking me on a different journey.

My career also changed as many people were drawn to me to end their own suffering. More than twenty-four years on the work has continued to grow, as have I. Working as a Self Empowerment Consultant and Trainer has been both a gift and blessing, to have worked with people from all walks of life, and professions from the armed forces, police, educators and their students, and the clergy to name a few. You see no matter who you are or what you do, we are all the same, we are all on the same journey. The only question is are we taking that journey consciously or unconsciously?

My life as I had known it had ended. However, there was this powerful knowing that all the endings were doorways to my new beginnings, and they were absolutely right for me.

My life continued to change as I was no longer the deeply unconscious person I used to be, although she did pop up at times. When I say pop up, she invariably appeared through the fearful thoughts. Unconscious thoughts such as 'how will I cope on my own,' but then those thoughts would be instantly seen and dissolved, sometimes they would express through the emotional and physical bodies, but only when I gave them enough attention, even then they could not stay for long.

I had seen Truth, now to living it. All that was stopping me was a single thought believed in any one moment. I had been given the tools within which to free myself, and my life became the practice ground within which to do just that. I continued growing into the awareness of my True Self through every questioned thought.

Increasingly I became the witness of those unconscious thoughts, which arose through fear. Fear that was imagined, fear that was a projection of the past into the future and typically had nothing to do with reality.

For me there was no sudden powerful awakening where the false self instantly ceased to exist. But rather I had begun a journey of Self Empowerment, one of realising the True Self, some might call this Self Realisation. The words to describe this are not important, only that in this lifetime, you experience this for yourself. The SEJ Process makes this possible, for everyone.

Chapter Nine

Why do we suffer?

We suffer quite simply because we genuinely believe our thoughts, and very often those thoughts oppose what is. Let us just look at a simple thought.

'Oh no, it's raining, why is it raining today when I need to go out.'

This thought is arguing with what is, the thought then triggers an emotional reaction, physical sensations and causes you to take action, all of which are disempowering and feel negative. The first unconscious action is often one of verbalising the situation that you perceive in the negative. Once you verbalise, as in our example 'Oh no it's raining, why is it raining today when I need to go out' you find yourself on a slippery slope, where one negative thought very rapidly leads to another. For example, 'I'm not going to bother going out now, I'll go for a walk another time with my friend.'

When we carefully look at this example, which is only about the weather, suffering is already happening because we are arguing with what is. When we argue with what is we take limiting actions. One limiting action then leads to another driven by limiting thoughts: it's a downward mental, emotional, physical, and vibrational spiral. Looking at this simple example, we can therefore begin to understand the untold suffering experienced, when life predictably brings other situations to us that might include unexpected change or loss.

Chapter Ten

It's a bad habit

Naively believing your thoughts is quite simply a bad habit. You may observe many people earnestly trying to change their unconscious thoughts and think positively, but if you have tried positive thinking, you will know it is limited in its success. Using our example, you might typically say 'Oh well it's okay that it's raining' but your negative emotions and physical sensations are telling a different story, you still feel annoyed and frustrated, and this is quite simply because you don't believe the positive thought. You can't seem to break the habit of believing the negative thought.

Therefore, we can only break the habit if we become conscious and practice self-enquiry. This way we come into alignment with our truthful thoughts and suffering ends. This is the only way to break the habit. By this I mean, you have questioned the thought and through the SEJ Process have sufficiently realised the reality of the situation, once reality is seen you no longer resist what is and the habit of unconsciously believing thoughts is broken. It's that simple.

Chapter Eleven

The mind can never see reality

The mind can never see reality. It merely reacts to stimuli as in our example, 'it's raining' and so you have a memory-based thought rise from within you about the rain. All thoughts are 'old news', they come from memory. Therefore, they rarely fit with what is happening in the present moment. You cannot genuinely appreciate the rain because you have typically learnt to react unfavourably, you have learnt to go into your mind for the possible answers. Mind does not have your answers; it only stores information.

Let us look at it this way. Imagine you have a filing cabinet filled with every experience you ever had, and from those experiences you promptly took on personal beliefs. Beliefs are of course simply constantly repeated thoughts, repeated often enough they are erroneously believed, and you identify with them, you claim them as yours, they are your thoughts and beliefs.

Now everyone naturally has a unique filing cabinet, let us say when you were 6 years old you were bitten by a dog, but your friend grew up with dogs and was always playing with them. When you were older, you were both out together and a dog came running towards you, your longtime friend bent down to greet the dog in a safe way, you on the other hand froze to the spot with paralysing fear, heart racing, screaming 'get it away.'

You believe, you both believe, they are your own reactions, however they are only memory-based thoughts that are typically working through you based upon stimuli, in this example the dog. So, because you genuinely believe your thoughts about the dog, emotions, physical sensations, and actions are all working through you, and you incorrectly identify with them as you. But what if this is untrue, what if it is as simple as stimuli triggers memory which replays through the mental, emotional, and physical bodies, and this memory is unreliable information because it is 'old news.' Well, this is exactly what happens.

You may be thinking there's nothing new here, cognitive therapy is based precisely upon this premise. And I agree, nothing new, but to me it was new when this conscious awareness came, I knew nothing of cognitive therapy, of how my body, mind and emotions were inextricably linked, this awareness came to me when I saw how stimuli triggered within me a reaction.

Where the SEJ Process differs tremendously from cognitive therapy, is that I absolutely realise, going back into the mind to problem solve is not the solution, it is obvious really when you think about it. Mind is the problem, and although you can reprogram the mind, what you reprogram it with still invariably comes from mind! What we are doing with the SEJ is going beyond mind.

With the SEJ you do not stop mind from offering its suggestions, which is all that it is doing when it offers you an unconscious memory-based thought in response to stimuli. However, because all thoughts come from memory, we must question their accuracy in relation to this present moment – reality. The SEJ process creates a framework for you to question thoughts to realise Truth.

We do not want to stop the mind from making its suggestions. It is extremely important we keep our minds agile, but we must also recognise its limitations, or to be more accurate our limitations in how we use our mind.

Let's carefully look at another example, if I get into my car, I need to know how to drive and this is where memory serves me well, getting into the car is the stimuli, memory appears in thoughts, emotions, physical sensations and so driving happens (action).

When we initially learn to drive, we need to input data into the mind (memory), so that knowing how to drive can be recalled when required. However, when I want to know for example, which job offer to take, this is where mind is severely limited. At this point a person will search their mind for reasons to take a particular job. They will analyse and make logical decisions coming to a conclusion. This is where a person's potential then becomes limited, for in essence, they are unquestionably hazarding a guess based on what they know (memory).

This is where the SEJ naturally comes into its power, through the process you can question all thoughts and in so doing you are led to Truth. The Truth is beyond anything the mind could possibly offer or imagine and is seldom the logical choice. As we then act from the realised Truth we are risen above our recurring cycles and bonds. Realising our highest potential and True Self, we become limitless rather than limited.

Chapter Twelve

Truth is who you are

Truth is in essence who you are. As stated earlier we genuinely believe we are our thoughts, emotions, and physical body. This is the three-body cycle we unconsciously live in. Truth, which we call the Spiritual body or Truth body in the process, is who you are. The three bodies of thoughts, emotions and physical sensations/actions are merely how Truth (you) expresses itself.

When you are working from the three lower bodies, (which is who you incorrectly believe you are), without any awareness of the Truth body, you are thinking your way through life. You are therefore expressing memory (old thoughts and beliefs) through the emotional and physical bodies.

As one would reasonably expect, it may not feel like memory because the people and events are often different, but the thoughts you experience in relation to these events are nevertheless memory-based. Therefore, although the events and people may inevitably change your reactions do not, they still come from memory. Only when you come from Truth, are you able to respond as the True Self.

The fundamental truth is you are never responding when you come from memory; you are typically reacting, re-enacting the past. This is why, for example in relationships, you keep experiencing the same disagreements with your partner. Or you leave one partner, meet someone new and in the new relationship the same issues arise. With depression, as in my own experience, you suffer recurring bouts of depression. Everyone is stuck in limiting unconscious cycles. In other words, you typically keep reacting to life in the same way, the same thoughts, triggering the same emotions, physical sensations and limiting reactions.

When Truth arose from within me with the thought 'I don't want to live like this' it changed my emotions, physical sensations and actions. The cycle was broken. Prior to this I was quite simply prepared to end my life because I genuinely believed the thought 'I don't want to live.'

Self-enquiry just happened within me, but generally this does not happen. Therefore, we have the SEJ Process. A self-enquiry process enabling you to access the Truth and live to your full potential, responding consciously to life rather than reacting (re-enacting the past).

Does it sound too simple that all you need to do is question your thoughts to be free and reach your full potential? Well in many respects it is simple, and life changing. What is not simple is doing self-enquiry without a comprehensive framework to use, as it is easy to slip back into your mind (personal memory). Yet once you use the SEJ, and you dedicate yourself to the practice of it, as 'every thought is up for questioning,' you too will find yourself in the place I found myself when I woke up to reality, self-enquiry will just work through you. The day will come when you will no longer work the process, but the process will work through you.

Chapter Thirteen

From unconscious to conscious living

Up until the time I woke up to truth I had no idea that I was living unconsciously. Indeed, how many of us think we are unconscious? I am sure most of you would say, as I did then, that you know exactly what you are thinking and doing.

But do you?

Here in lies the problem, we don't know we live unconsciously. In other words, we are constantly reacting from memory in relation to the present. Therefore, we never experience life exactly as it is.

To move from unconscious to conscious living, we must realise that all thoughts come from memory, there are never any new thoughts. When a thought is repeated enough times, it becomes a belief. These past thoughts (beliefs) are triggered by present life events, therefore, as we live our life, we essentially re-live the past.

Because your thoughts appear relevant to the present, you genuinely believe them and this is why they go unquestioned; relevant they may be, but truthful and accurate they are not. Therefore, when you listen to the memory-based thoughts triggered in the present, you serve only to repeat the past.

Let's look at an example, have you ever had the same repetitive disagreement with a partner, friend, or colleague? Every time they do or say a certain thing, you respond in the same way: same thoughts, feelings (emotions) and actions. E.g., they say or do something you disagree with, you get upset and angry, then have the same argument that you had with them previously.

Does your response to them feel relevant? Yes, otherwise, you wouldn't be responding in the way you are.

Does your repeated response to them alter the situation? No, otherwise, you wouldn't repeat the same argument over and over.

This is quite simply because you are not responding to the situation. To respond is to be conscious and view the situation with fresh eyes, as if for the first time, with no memory of the past interfering. You have not been responding you have been merely reacting, in a continued reactive state re-enacting the past.

To live consciously, we must question all our thoughts; the problem is knowing how to do this in a conscious way. Simply questioning thoughts is not enough, for you will be questioning them with more thoughts that come from memory, and so will only access more memory-based thoughts. This is why we must access Truth in the form of thought, and why knowing how to instantly access Truth in a structured way, will ensure you do not fall victim to more unconscious thoughts.

When you're conscious, you will be free of the mind's memory and imaginings (past and future), but as I said earlier how do you know when you're conscious? As you may absolutely believe you already are. Only through questioning all thoughts will you undoubtedly know.

Surely it is too much to ask to question all thoughts, as there's thousands of them a day. Depending upon which research you view the average number of thoughts a person thinks a day is 6,000 of which 90% are repetitive. In my awareness the 90% is an underestimate, but let's say this is accurate. That means: 90% of your thoughts come from memory, therefore 90% of your day you are re-enacting the past over and over, and so 90% of the time you are unconscious!

So, where within the 90% do you begin? As you start to use the SEJ Process, you will typically begin questioning the obvious unconscious thoughts, then the less obvious unconscious thoughts will become more obvious to you. Or to put it another way, you will become more conscious to your unconscious 'self'.

I recall one training event in a business setting, where one of the employees was quite adamant their life was fine and indeed, they were already happy. To them their thoughts were conscious. Yet when we examined more closely, (which didn't take long), they definitely were not conscious and weren't therefore living to their full potential. There was evidently lack in many areas of their life, unfulfilled both personally and professionally. Can you see how the mind lies; how easy it is to be deceived by yourself? It repeatedly lies to you and others. We are blind to truth and reality.

To begin your journey of Self empowerment you too just need to start by considering where there is lack in your life, your emotions will guide you. If you feel sad, upset, and worried about something, there is lack. Look to find where you are not reaching your full potential, the stories that your mind tells about this and the negative emotions you feel. Start there.

In the Appendix there is a list of 'Collective Beliefs' about key aspects of life, to support and assist you in identifying beliefs that you can begin to put through the SEJ Process. Through the SEJ Training we carefully explore this in a lot more detail.

I highly recommend you take some time to read this chapter again and willingly let the reality and truth of what I have said sink in. For the mind may dismiss being unconscious for at least 90% of the day, believing this may apply to other people but not yourself. The reality is people tend to only become conscious when something deeply profound or shocking happens that forces them to become fully present. Until then unconscious repeating of the past is happening virtually every moment, when you drive your car, speak with a customer, chat with your children, brush your teeth, go to work, clean your home, engage with a friend...

Chapter Fourteen

Truth or intuition?

At this point you might be thinking that Truth sounds very much like intuition.

This is not the case, allow me to elaborate.

Intuition might otherwise be described as an inner voice or gut instinct; I have even heard it referred to as an internal Satnav. It is a voice within that guides you in an inspired way. It is in essence something that is seen as separate from you that you look to access or receive guidance from. Some call it the Higher Self, which leads to the belief in a 'lower self' or ego. In essence this is true however, whilst you believe in accessing your intuition you actually reinforce the separation and belief of a Higher and lower self.

The Truth is more than this, it is the ability to access an inner voice that gives direction, but this voice is you, it is who you are in Truth, the best way to understand it is through our SEJ quote.

"Self Empowerment is the realisation of the True Self beyond the mind. This realisation puts you in touch with a

Self that is free of limitations, free of fearful thoughts and feelings, free to respond to life rather than react, free to reach your full potential. The Self Empowerment Journey – SEJ is a process that takes you to this realisation."

So, we can see from the quote that using the SEJ Process, enables you to dissolve that which you believe you are and become SELF Realised. Here Truth speaks freely through you, as you all the time, instead of seeking your intuition which can be very hit or miss.

I have found many people struggle to know when intuition or their own mind is speaking. Through using the SEJ you will find there is no struggle or separation. If we were to use the words Higher and lower self, you might say you dissolve all thoughts that cause you to believe in a lower self and therefore you can only be your Higher Self. In this there is nothing to be separate from, you are whole.

Chapter Fifteen

Thoughts have no power

Thoughts have no power over you until you voluntarily give them your focused attention. The more attention you award them the more intense they naturally become. The problem is once a thought becomes a belief (through continued focus upon the thought), it feels all but impossible to overcome and stop focusing on it, a belief can feel very real and insurmountable.

Have you ever noticed you have many thoughts through-out the day which you don't give your attention to, then suddenly that one thought appears in your mind, and you focus your attention upon it? Why? Because you genuinely believe it, it absolutely is that simple and this is why we have the SEJ, to question those thoughts believed.

Carefully consider, if you constantly believed the thought 'I'm not good enough' what would this do to you mentally, emotionally, and physically? You may become overwhelmed with life and never really live to your full potential. It is the difference between getting the perfect job/relationship, etc. and not, because when you believe thoughts such as 'I'm not good enough' it must become a reality for you.

A belief is simply a constantly repeated thought that you give power to by placing your attention on it. People have typically given their attention to such beliefs for years and so the idea of questioning them seems ridiculous, as the mind will give evidence in the form of more thoughts based on your experiences to support the belief. It will justly say the considered belief is true because your life experiences prove it.

> *"You believe the experience which reinforces the belief, change the belief change the experience."*

As my quote says you believe the experience, because you cannot yet see the experience is simply a manifestation of the belief. Therefore, to change your experiences you MUST change your beliefs first. But what we have been typically taught is to change our outside reality, when it is the internal reality, we must change.

Consider that you only ever experience life inside of you. You can have two people in the same life situation, let's say at a fairground, one person might find the rides exhilarating, another terrifying. The situation has not changed, but how it is experienced is different for each person and is based upon the individual beliefs held by them.

Thoughts appear only because of stimuli, in other words to further our example. A friend mentions going to a fairground, you are not even there and yet your mind is already running a story about it, the story might go something like this:

'No, absolutely not, I hate fairground rides. I don't mind hook-a-duck but that's about it, can't we do something else'?

As soon as you give the personal story your focused attention, your emotional state changes, maybe fear, anxiety rises within you, the body reacts to the thought because even though you are only talking about the fairground your emotions and body don't know any difference between the thoughts you believe and reality. Therefore, the physical body becomes tense, maybe you begin to sweat or feel sick, and of course then any action you take is based upon the thought believed.

Until you become conscious of your thoughts and question them, you will be a victim to them, and more so believe you are them. In truth, thoughts have no power over you, on realising this we must carefully consider who we might be without the thought, and that we are not our thoughts.

The personal stories your mind is telling about you, others and life quite simply are unlikely to be true. So, who you think you are, and who you actually are, the absolute truth is what we invariably begin to unravel when practicing assiduously the SEJ. The fundamental question of 'Who Am I?' will naturally arise as a consequence of doing the SEJ.

Chapter Sixteen

You cannot control your thoughts

You cannot control your thoughts, but then again do you really want to? You see, your mind offers you suggestions in the form of thoughts, as said earlier based upon stimuli. Let's re-visit the driving example. I need to drive somewhere; the stimuli are knowing I need to get somewhere and my car. I need my mind to remind me how to open the door, use the gears, and so on. Without the ability to think I cannot function.

Therefore, never seek to control your thoughts instead question them, for as you now know, all thoughts are memory-based, and we need our memories. We need the knowledge held within our memories, and we need it to appear at the perfect time. Therefore, stimuli will trigger your memory-based thoughts in the attempt to sufficiently answer the questions stimuli presents. But if we have been programmed inappropriately, what memory gives us in the form of a thought will only limit us if believed.

What do I mean by programming? Imagine, for example, you were sick on the bus as a child. After this experience whenever you had to travel by bus, you began to feel sick and fearful. Even the thought of a bus would make you feel anxious and sick and so you wouldn't go on the bus. This would truly limit a person's life.

But there is more to the SEJ than even this, we don't want incorrect programmed reactions to hinder us, but neither do we want what may appear positive programmed reactions to hinder us. What we do want is to be able to seek truth, and this can never come from memory. My memory is remarkable when reminding me how to drive the car, but memory might also tell me which route to take. This is where mind becomes severely limited, because the route we followed yesterday might not be the best route for today, and this is where Truth comes in, as you question all thoughts it allows space for Truth to naturally rise from within, something the mind can never do is give you Truth.

Truth is not restricted to this moment; it is multi-dimensional and therefore able to direct you to the best reality where you can reach your full potential. Only your mind is frozen in time; you are not, and you are not your mind, even though you may think so.

Chapter Seventeen

Most people believe they are their thoughts

Most people genuinely believe they are their thoughts, body, and emotions, and yet if you consider what was given earlier with our Fairground example, merely believing a thought triggered an emotional and physical reaction, without the person even being at the Fairground.

In the next moment you typically change your thought and suddenly you experience a different emotion and bodily sensation. Therefore, it is impossible to be your thoughts, body, and emotions. You are the one believing the thought, and as you believe the thought you set in motion the emotional and physical reactions.

It's easy to understand why we falsely believe we are our thoughts because they seldom leave us alone, you tell yourself not to think of something and there you are again thinking about it, you are completely identified with them. They are your thoughts for sure, but remember thoughts are simply triggered because of stimuli. If I erased your memory, you would still be here.

The fundamental question then is 'who am I', or 'who would I be without this thought?' You will find out as soon as you question your thought. You know who you are when you believe the thought, as you unwittingly become the thought naming it as 'me and my life.' When you question the thought, you become something else. You are constantly evolving as you question the thoughts believed, unless you are stuck believing thoughts about yourself, others, and life, in which case you get older, but your experience of life stays the same.

We are meant to evolve into higher states of awareness, not just get older, yet this can only happen if we remain open. Remaining open can only happen if we practice self-enquiry, in other words question ALL our thoughts.

If you are willing to question all your thoughts (especially those you absolutely believe), you will absolutely see by using the process that you no longer need to desperately try and let go of your thoughts, which never works, because they will let go of you.

The thoughts are questioned, and they let go of you. You see, you cannot ever let go of them. It is impossible as we said earlier, thoughts can even hound us into submission of a lesser experience of self, others, and life. When we do the process and meet our thoughts on neutral ground, they completely dissolve, only then are you able to experience who you truly are beyond the thought.

Chapter Eighteen

You are a storyteller

You are telling a story about other people situations yourself, and life. You are telling a wonderful story and unwittingly playing your part in it. Question is, are you enjoying the story you are telling? Check out how you feel most of the time, this will give an indication of the type of story you are telling, is it a horror movie, are you filled with fear, or is it a love story, filled with overwhelming joy?

You may not have control over what appears in your present moment experience, but what you do have control over, is the story you tell about it, initially to yourself and then to others. For the one that questions their thoughts, even the most horrific experiences can be seen through the eyes of peace, even joy and love.

As you do the SEJ, you eventually come to see everything in your unique experience reflects your own thinking. What you think and ultimately believe about life and others is in you too. The world mirrored back to us is merely a projection of our beliefs.

We need to tell a new story, one that both enables and empowers. Since time began, people have tried changing the world, so that they can be happy, inevitably failing to see that this can only happen if the internal experience is changed. We have certainly advanced in several areas such as technology, however when it comes to progressively developing into conscious human beings in which we no longer suffer, in this there has been little to no progress. Just look and see, how is the world doing? What is the world mirroring back to us?

Humanity's thinking is backwards, to move forwards we MUST do the internal work, to change our internal 'story' and then our external will change. The SEJ gives you the framework for self-enquiry to happen, to change the internal so your external changes.

Chapter Nineteen

Positive thinking and willpower do not work

Have you ever tried telling yourself a positive thought and no matter how many times you positively affirm it your emotions and body are telling a different story? In essence the emotional and physical body do not believe you because a positive thought does not have the power to dissolve a belief, only self-enquiry can do that.

Equally no matter how determined you are to change your beliefs and behaviours using willpower, does it actually happen? No, not when a belief is embedded in the subconscious. This is good news, for you do not need to rely on willpower to experience change.

What is essential is the sincere desire to create change, to end your suffering, only then will the SEJ Process work for you. You must have attained to a place in your life where you no longer wish to suffer, where you are prepared to accept personal responsibility. Or perhaps you know there is more to life than what you are currently experiencing but you cannot seem to create change. Maybe you have even asked the questions 'what is life about,' or 'who am I?' At these moments, the SEJ is for you, and your job is to do the Process.

I can share with you what I know, and it works, but you must make it work for you by practicing assiduously and dedicating yourself to the process. If the thought of practicing and dedicating yourself to the process stirs up negative thoughts and feelings, then do the SEJ on those thoughts, so you are free to practice and dedicate yourself to your Self Empowerment Journey.

Chapter Twenty

The SEJ Process

The SEJ Process is simple and easy to use, with just four steps to work through. Step 1 is problem focused and Steps 2 through to 4 are solution focused, it is, therefore, a solution focused process, which of itself is extremely empowering.

Step 1 Self Awareness is about recalling a situation that typically caused or is in this present moment causing you to suffer. At this step you gather information that will reveal to you the source of the problem.

Step 2 SELF Regulation, here we begin to find Truth, the conscious solution to the problem.

Step 3 SELF Confidence, now we discover evidence and projections to support and expand upon this realised Truth.

Step 4 SELF Empowerment, here we test the solution. There is no waiting for results they are immediate.

The SEJ Process works 100% of the time, you simply need to genuinely commit to doing the process, which once practiced can be done in moments, but to start with may take a little longer as you use the SEJ Worksheet to develop your practice. Eventually, you will not need the worksheet as you will no longer be working the process, the process will work through you.

Every time you complete a worksheet; you are opening the mental, emotional, and physical bodies to the correct way of working. (More detailed information on this is shared in the SEJ Training).

If by Step 4 you have not achieved a state of empowerment, then it will purely be because you have not completed the worksheet correctly. The primary reason is that you will be completing the worksheet from thought (memory) rather than from the deeper dimension within, Truth.

REMEMBER

The SEJ is only going to work for you if you are ready to see the Truth and accept full responsibility for your own life. You must be open to the following:

1. No one is going to fix you – you are the one you have been always looking for.
2. All suffering is happening inside of you – ownership and personal responsibility are essential.
3. You must do the process for it to work. Don't let your mind talk you out of doing the SEJ. Mind has its own agenda; follow the voice of Truth.

You need to be, if not already, able to take personal responsibility. Not blaming life and others, at least open to see that no one is to blame for how you are feeling and the actions you take. Open to the experience that all suffering happens within you, and therefore freedom from suffering comes effortlessly as you do the work on yourself.

A last point, the SEJ Process is extremely powerful and yet wonderfully simple to use. Do not confuse its simplicity with it's potential to transform you and your life, dare I say it, to even produce miracles!

Chapter Twenty-one

How to complete the SEJ Worksheet

In this chapter I am going to show you how to complete the SEJ Worksheet with an example. As we go through the example you may wish to complete your own worksheet. It will help you to understand the process. Please take your time, there is no need to rush the process.

SEJ Worksheet

STEP ONE: Self Awareness

Situation...

Firstly, I would like you to recall a situation that caused you to suffer, maybe you felt distressed, hurt, angry, sad, disappointed, or upset etc.

Once you have this situation, I would like you to just note it here on the Worksheet:

EXAMPLE: My boss wants me to deliver a report by the end of the day.

The Story...

Next write down exactly what happened, write down the 'story' your mind is telling about the situation. It is extremely important you do not censor the 'story'; your thoughts may be very dark, petty, unkind, or judgmental. This is OK they are just thoughts; it is not who you are, but it is important you write down the thoughts exactly as they appear in your mind.

Take your time. Step one is the only opportunity you will get to offload the problem onto paper, so get it all out of your mind and put it down on the worksheet. If you run out of space, write on the back of the worksheet. Go for it!

EXAMPLE: "Who does my boss think he is demanding I write this report to suit his schedule, what about mine! I need to pick the kids up. I can't be late. I hate this job. I hate my boss! I can't wait to leave here. I'd leave today but I can't afford it. It's not fair nothing ever goes my way. I'm so tired of trying. I feel like giving up. I can't be bothered, let him sack me if he wants, serve him right, he can do his own bloody report!"

List Your Thoughts... Once the story has been written list the thoughts that grab your attention the most, probably those that cause you the most distress.

EXAMPLE:

1. I hate this job.
2. I hate my boss.
3. It's not fair nothing ever goes my way.
4. I am so tired of trying.
5. I feel like giving up.

From the above list extract just one thought you would like to work on, one thought = one worksheet. We are now going to look at how just one thought can impact us emotionally, physically (bodily sensations and actions), and spiritually.

At this point let's look at the spiritual, the spiritual can be viewed quite simply as being either open or closed to life / situation / person. Let's look at our example.

Mental: The thought I believe is...Write here the thought you believe. (The thought you have chosen to work on).

I hate my boss.

Emotional: The emotions I experience when I believe this thought are...Note here your emotions when you believe this thought - JUST THIS THOUGHT not the whole story.

Angry, frustrated.

Physical: When I believe this thought my bodily sensations are… What are the sensations in your body when you believe this thought?

Jaw clenched.

Physical Action: When I believe this thought my actions are… What action do you take / not take when you believe this thought?

I reluctantly do the report, I don't make much effort.

Spiritual: When I believe this thought I am closed to… Write here who or what you feel closed to, e.g., life / the situation / person / everything?

Closed to my boss.

STEP TWO SELF Regulation

Einstein realised the same powerful truth as I. He said,

> *"I think 99 times and find nothing.*
> *I stop thinking, swim in silence and*
> *the Truth comes to me."*

This is what we begin to do at Step 2, we go in search of Truth, and we have two ways of doing this. Firstly, there is what we call the 'Sitting in Silence' practice, this simply requires you to sit and greet the thought chosen, our example was 'I hate my boss.' Sit with your own example.

As you sit with the thought you stop thinking, in other words you don't run with this thought or add new thoughts to it, you simply sit and remain open observing the thought with no judgment. In this open state a Truth, (which appears as a thought), will rise from within you, if you are open. This takes practice as initially mind will also offer thoughts; you will know the difference because a Truthful thought will resonate. If you are struggling, we have another option.

Climb the ladder of Truth: If you are closed for whatever reason, and so the Truth doesn't rise from within you simply 'climb the ladder of Truth.' So here we play around with some opposites, again using our example this might look like:

I hate my boss.
Opposites:
I love my boss
I like my boss
I don't hate my boss

Continue until a truth is reached. How do you know it's a Truth? It MUST resonate, you will feel it very powerfully. If the new thought seems obvious, or too simple, don't question it, just note the difference in how you feel, if your emotions have changed to more empowering and positive emotions you are on the right track. When it resonates it will be a 'light bulb moment.'

Next you complete the 4 bodies again. Notice the shift in all 4 bodies. If they have not moved to better feeling emotions and actions then re-do step 2, you are probably still coming from mind.

Mental: My Truth is... Write here the truthful thought that rises from within.

I don't hate my boss.

Emotional: The emotions I experience when I allow space for this Truth are... Note here your changed emotions when you clearly see the Truth.

Relieved, at ease.

Physical: With this Truth my bodily sensations are... Observe your body, notice the change in bodily sensations as the Truth settles within you.

Jaw is relaxed. I feel less tense all over.

Physical Action: With this Truth my actions
are...What action do you take / not take when you listen
to Truth?

I do the report to the best of my ability.

Spiritual: With this Truth I am open to...There should
now be a shift from being closed to open. Do you feel
open or closed to life / the situation / person?

When we are open, we are once again able to function
fully in all 4 bodies and consequently experience not only
our limitless potential, but all that life has to offer us that
we cannot see or experience when closed. There is also a
vibrational shift where we are now allowing the
manifestation of our full potential in all areas of our life.

Open to the situation and my boss.

STEP THREE SELF Confidence

We are now at Step 3, which is about developing
confidence in your TRUE SELF. For a long time, you may
have been listening to and believing limiting thoughts
which you identified with, e.g., a thought says, 'I'm
useless' and you believe that of yourself, we call this the
false self.

At this Step you quite simply look for evidence and mirrors

(projections) to support the Truth which has risen from your True Self. The evidence and mirrors must again rise from within you, they MUST NOT come from mind.

To gather your evidence, sit as in Step 2 and allow the Truth to rise from within you. The evidence is a continuation of the Truth realised at Step 2. A good starting point is to add the word 'because' at the end of the new realised Truth and continue from there.

'Mirrors' are thoughts and beliefs we project onto others, and so we need to claim them back for ourselves. Mirrors tend to show themselves as you go deeply into the evidence. They initially appear in the 'story' at Step 1. Here are some examples of mirrors:

She's angry. The mirror is I'm angry.
He's jealous. The mirror is I'm jealous.
They don't listen. The mirror is I don't listen.

You can add 'because' at the end of the mirror to create space for Truth to elaborate.

As you can see all the examples are brought back to ourselves. It is essential we own these mirrors as part of our empowerment and journey towards unity consciousness.

The mirrors don't always relate to the situation you're working on, although they can. Let's say your story is about a jealous colleague. You may absolutely know you are not jealous of them, but as you allow Truth to rise from within, you are able to own you are jealous of your sister **because** she gets more attention than you.

The story of the sister that gets more attention than you is a potential new worksheet. As all thoughts are up for questioning.

Look at our example, mirrors are underlined in the text.

Write your evidence and highlight your mirrors here:

I don't hate my boss because...well I simply don't. He is really very generous; he does show gratitude for the work I do, and he does take the time to say thank you. Also, he's only asking me to do my job, which I am great at, that's a compliment.

I said I hate my boss, but I realise the mirror here is that the person 'I hate' although strong words, is myself, not my boss. I hate myself; I know this sounds negative but it's not, this is what I have been doing to myself, it's how I have been feeling about myself! I hate myself for not speaking up as he probably doesn't realise or consider I have other commitments, that I often do need to leave work on time. He probably doesn't know this because I give him mixed messages.

I wish I could speak up more. It's not his problem it's mine. He's only asking me to do my job. I need to be clearer about my commitments and when I can and cannot work. I'm projecting onto him how I feel about myself within the situation and my inability to say what I want to say. He said what he wanted to say, I simply did nothing. I need to speak up and respond to his requests appropriately. He doesn't know my work schedule; he couldn't possibly know it would be tight for me to complete by the end of the day!

I always believed <u>my boss brought this situation to me, but the mirror is I bring it to myself as I am the one that is demanding, not him</u>. I am demanding with my thoughts and attitude towards my boss. He's not doing anything wrong. I will put through another worksheet not being able to speak up for myself.

Once again, we go through the 4 bodies. This time choose either a Truth from Step 3 (as in our example) or if the most empowering Truth is still the one at Step 2 you can use that one again.

Mental: My Truth is... Write here the most empowering Truth.

I bring these situations to myself.

Emotional: My emotions are…Note here your emotions, see how they have changed now you have accessed the Truth.

I feel really empowered, almost strong, happy even.

Physical: My physical sensations are…Note here your physical sensations, again notice how they have changed now you have accessed the Truth.

Smiling, tingly.

Physical Action: My actions are… Note here what actions you take now you have accessed the Truth. Notice how your actions change the direction of your life. No matter how small the action is, all actions create a ripple effect and evidence your vibration.

I want to be able to speak up for myself. I want to take responsibility for my actions and stop blaming others. Before I felt powerless because I couldn't change my boss, I kept trying to change him, but it was me that needed to change all along and this I have the power to do. This is what I am going to do as I speak up for myself and stop trying to change him.

Spiritual: I am open to... Notice how you are now open. State in what ways you are now open.

I feel open to my boss and the situation, but most of all to myself. Prior to doing this, all I could see was what I was projecting onto my boss. I couldn't even see my part in the situation at all. I was shocked when I realised that I hated myself, and yet it was such a powerful life changing moment for me. It is hard to put into words how I feel, it's as if all the anger and frustration has just fallen away and I can see clearly for the first time. Thank you.

STEP FOUR SELF Empowerment

Finally, at Step 4 we test the original thought believed to see what has changed. At this step you are now empowered and able to take different actions. These will impact your life positively and enable you to reach your full potential.

Mental:
The thought I believed at Step 1 was...

I hate my boss.

Emotional:
My emotions have changed to…

I just feel still, calm.

Physical:
My physical sensations have changed to…

Nothing is happening my body is just resting.

Physical Action:
My actions have changed to…

The thought is no longer true for me so no action to take.

Spiritual: This statement is true for me. 'I am no longer closed to… I am open to…(life / situation / person)

I am no longer closed to my boss; I feel open to everything.

Outcomes: To complete Step 4 we write out the outcomes to the situation.

Immediate Outcomes: (Internal Situation) Immediate Outcomes will be the change to your thoughts, emotions, physical sensations, actions, and being open.

Calm, body resting, open to life, everything. Change of attitude and perception. I can see everything clearly, or rather truthfully instead of what I think is happening.

Life Outcomes: (External Situation) Life Outcomes will be evident in the moment if the SEJ is done as the situation arises or appears later if the process is done retrospectively. You can keep adding to the life outcomes over a period of days, weeks, even years as you see the ripple effect and profound impact taking a different action can have in altering your life.

I did another SEJ Worksheet and realised I can speak up for myself, I do it often enough in other situations, I just didn't believe I could at work!

I week later:

My boss asked me today to complete some work before I left. I responded with OK, because I could stay later, I even wanted to stay to complete it. I know if I couldn't have stayed, I would have just as easily been able to say no.

18 months later:

I stayed in a job which I love, and I am appreciated. I found my voice which led to a promotion and a wage increase. I am so glad I didn't leave!

As you can see from this example the results are immediate, and equally continue to unfold with a life enhancing ripple effect. The realised Truth results in a change of perception influencing future outcomes to similar situations.

Every time we act there is an impact upon our own life and the lives of those around us. As we take personal responsibility through the SEJ for our thoughts, feelings, and actions, we are truly able to become the master of our destiny and live to our full potential moment to moment.

When you first begin to practice the SEJ Process almost all your worksheets will be retrospective. However, as you commit to your SEJ practice you will do the SEJ the moment a disempowering thought appears in your mind. Dedication to the practice of the SEJ is the key to success.

Chapter Twenty-two

SEJ worksheet examples

I have chosen 3 worksheets to share with you, each exploring typical situations and beliefs that many of us have. As you read through the worksheets why not consider your own thoughts and reactions and try out the SEJ for yourself.

Worksheet 1

HEALTH EXAMPLE – A client that believed what others and the mirrors in life were showing her, rather than following her own truth.

I love this example because not only does it show how questioning your thoughts can change your physical body / health. But it also shows how easy it is to 'steal' your beliefs from others.

Remember a belief is just a constantly repeated thought, of which no thoughts are new because they are memory based; at some point you stole them from another, no thought is ever yours. Look at how you steal your thoughts, try it out, see if you can find one thought that is yours, by yours I mean unique to you that does not come from your True Self.

STEP ONE: Self Awareness

Situation...

Recall a situation that caused you to suffer, maybe you felt distressed, hurt, angry, sad, disappointed, or upset. Once you have this situation note it here:

Health issue – I have a condition that is affecting the muscles in my body, so I take steroids.

The Story…

Write here the 'story' your mind is telling about the situation. It is important you do not censor your thoughts, write them exactly as they appear to you, no matter how dark, petty, unkind, or judgmental they are.

I'm really fed up with being on these steroids, I don't want to take them any longer, I didn't want to take these tablets in the first place. I feel really dependent on them. They're making me put on weight.

I have been on these steroids for over 4 years now, the doctor recommends I use them. I am so dependent on taking these tablets to keep the pain and stiffness out of my muscles. Without taking these tablets I am in so much pain just combing my hair, making a cup of tea, walking up the stairs to go to the bathroom and doing many other simple tasks around the home, if I don't take them.

I feel so tired and depressed when I think about taking these steroids indefinitely. If I just miss taking one of them, it leaves me in so much pain and stiffness in my muscles. I wish I could do without them for good. People say I won't ever get off the steroids.

List your thoughts...

Once the story has been written list the thoughts that grab your attention.

1. I don't want to take them any longer.

2. I didn't want to take them in the first place.

3. I am so dependent on taking these tablets.

4. Without taking these tablets I am in so much pain.

5. I feel so tired and depressed.

6. I wish I could do without taking them for good.

From the above list extract just one thought you would like to work on and put that thought through the 4 bodies.

Mental: The thought I believe is...

I am so dependent on taking these tablets.

Emotional: The emotions I experience when I believe this thought are...

Depressed and saddened.

Physical: When I believe this thought my bodily sensations are...

Drained and my fists are clenched.

Physical Action: When I believe this thought my actions are...

Withdrawn from life and worry about

taking more of the tablets.

Spiritual: When I believe this thought I am closed to...

Closed to life.

STEP TWO SELF Regulation

Sit in Silence and greet the thought you believe. Remember as you sit with the thought you stop thinking, in other words you do not run with this thought or add new thoughts to it, you simply remain open, observing the thought with no judgment. In this open state a Truth will rise from within you.

Or...

Climb the ladder of Truth!

List some opposites until a thought resonates with you.

_____

_____

_____

_____

_____

_____

Mental: My Truth is…

I'm not dependent on taking these tablets.

Emotional: The emotions I experience when I allow space for this Truth are…

Happy and joyful.

Physical: With this Truth my bodily sensations are…

Energised.

Physical Action: With this Truth my actions are…

To start decreasing my tablets.

Spiritual: With this Truth I am open to…

Life.

STEP THREE SELF Confidence

We are now at Step 3, and here you quite simply look for **evidence and mirrors** to support your new Truth. These must again rise from within you, they MUST NOT come from mind. Simply sit and allow this to happen. A good starting point is to add the word 'because' at the end of the new realised Truth. Remember 'mirrors' are thoughts we project onto others, and so we need to claim them back for ourselves. Mirrors tend to show themselves as you go deeply into the evidence.

Write your evidence and highlight your mirrors here:

I'm not dependent on taking these tablets because I was given them to relax the pain and stiffness in my muscles that was restricting my movements, which they have done. I'm not dependent because if I begin to decrease them steadily my body will not have to depend on them so much until such a time when I will do without them. I'm not dependent because I can do without them because I realise that I'm not the same as everyone else, I know my own Self, I just know I can come off the tablets, I know my own body. I don't have to depend on them.

I realise people are mirroring back to me my own unquestioned thoughts, that I was <u>dependent, in pain, tired and depressed</u>, but these were just my thoughts being given back to me as I watched others with the same condition.

Life was mirroring back to me exactly what I was feeling and thinking, not the truth.

I realise that what I see in another is not necessarily my truth, I have taken on other people's thoughts and beliefs that I wasn't going to ever get off the steroids.

Once again, we go through the 4 bodies. This time choose either a Truth from Step 3 or if the most empowering Truth is still the one at Step 2 you can use this one again.

Mental: My Truth is…

I'm not dependent on taking these tablets.

Emotional: My emotions are…

Excited.

Physical: My physical sensations are…

Body feels light.

Physical Action: My actions are…

To start decreasing my tablets.

Spiritual: I am open to…

Life.

STEP FOUR SELF Empowerment

Test the original thought believed to see what's changed.

Mental:
The thought I believed at Step 1 was…

I am so dependent on taking these tablets.

Emotional:
My emotions have changed to…

Happy

Physical:
My physical sensations have changed to…

Laughing

Physical Action:
My actions have changed to…

Stillness, nothing to do.

Spiritual: This statement is true for me. 'I am no longer closed to… I am open to... (life / the situation / person).

I am no longer closed to life and my situation; I am open to all of life.

Outcomes: To complete Step 4 we write out the outcomes to the situation.

Immediate Outcomes: (Internal Situation) Immediate Outcomes will be the change to your thoughts, emotions, physical sensations, actions, and being open.

I immediately laughed because of the freedom that was given back to me in no longer being dependent on the steroids. I also felt still with an openness to life, I felt open to what life had given me. I realise how being on the steroids have restricted my life. I also feel open to others suffering the condition with no judgements.

Life Outcomes: (External Situation) Life Outcomes will be evident in the moment if the SEJ is done as the situation arises or appear later if the process is done retrospectively.

Beginning with my new thought, *'I'm not dependent on taking these tablets,'* I began to gradually decrease the number of tablets (guided by the Doctor) I was taking until I wasn't taking any at all. I have been free from taking any tablets at all for over 2 years, and with the continual use of doing the SEJ process I have never felt better.

Worksheet 2

OWNING OUR BEHAVIOURS EXAMPLE – When a lecturer's buttons were pushed, she reacted to her student. Once she owned the Truth, she felt immensely grateful and was able to address her own behaviours.

The SEJ is all about ownership and personal responsibility, suffering begins and ends inside of us, therefore the work to change our experience of life must be done within us.

STEP ONE: Self Awareness

Situation...

Recall a situation that caused you to suffer, maybe you felt distressed, hurt, angry, sad, disappointed, or upset. Once you have this situation note it here:

A student came to talk to me as she has been emailing me and I haven't responded.

The Story... Write here the 'story' your mind is telling about the situation. It is important you don't censor your thoughts, write them exactly as they appear to you, no matter how dark, petty, unkind, or judgmental they are.

What do you want? I don't know who you are. What? I don't understand what you are saying I don't remember you sending me any emails. You keep rabbiting on and on... What, how dare you say I'm too busy to speak with you? I'm so cross with you. Of course, I am busy I have a lot of stuff to do, and I don't have time for this. How dare you say I am too busy!

List your thoughts…

Once the story has been written list the thoughts that grab your attention.

1. I don't know who you are.

2. How dare you say I'm too busy!

3. What do you want?

4. I don't have time for this.

5. I have a lot of stuff to do.

From the above list extract just one thought you would like to work on and put that thought through the 4 bodies.

Mental: The thought I believe is…

How dare you say I'm too busy.

Emotional: The emotions I experience when I believe this thought are… REMEMBER TO FOCUS ON JUST THIS ONE THOUGHT NOT THE WHOLE STORY.

Angry, irritated.

Physical: When I believe this thought my bodily sensations are…

Frowning, body tense.

Physical Action: When I believe this thought my actions are…

Speaking loudly and making myself bigger and leaning over them.

Spiritual: When I believe this thought I am closed to…

Her and also to myself.

STEP TWO SELF Regulation

Sit in Silence and greet the thought you believe. Remember as you sit with the thought you stop thinking, in other words you do not run with this thought or add new thoughts to it, you simply remain open, observing the thought with no judgment. In this open state a Truth will rise from within you.

Or...

Climb the ladder of Truth!

List some opposites until a thought resonates with you.

How dare I say I'm too busy.

How true when you say that I'm too busy.

_____

_____

Mental: My Truth is...

How true when you say that I'm too busy.

Emotional: The emotions I experience when I allow space for this Truth are...

Humble and grateful.

Physical: With this Truth my bodily sensations are...

Body feels still.

Physical Action: With this Truth my actions are...

Fall silent, sit back.

Spiritual: With this Truth I am open to...

Her and myself

STEP THREE SELF Confidence

We are now at Step 3, and here you quite simply look for **evidence and mirrors** to support your new Truth. These must again rise from within you, they MUST NOT come from mind. Simply sit and allow this to happen. A good starting point is to add the word 'because' at the end of the new realised Truth. Remember 'mirrors' are thoughts we project onto others, and so we need to claim them back for ourselves. Mirrors tend to show themselves as you go deeply into the evidence.

Write your evidence and highlight your mirrors here:

How true you say that I'm too busy because actually she came to speak to me. Out of her perseverance, she came to speak with me, so she can have this issue sorted out. She took the trouble and guts to say that I am too busy even though she may find it a challenge to say that 'you are too busy to speak with me' to a lecturer. She took the trouble to say to me that 'you are too busy.'

I wasn't angry with her for saying that I was too busy. I was angry with her because she dared to point out the truth. I accused her of 'rabbiting on' but I was too busy, too busy listening to my mind as it

<u>was 'rabbiting on.'</u> She was the one who was honest. She was the one who could see the truth. Now I understand it was my error. She was being honest and pointed out something; it triggered a button in me because I didn't like the fact that she dared to point something that I hadn't spotted or accepted in myself that was what made me cross. <u>I was cross with myself,</u> (not her), for not daring to accept that I did not take my responsibility.... she took the trouble to tell me the truth.

Once again, we go through the 4 bodies. This time choose either a Truth from Step 3 or if the most empowering Truth is still the one at Step 2 you can use this one again.

Mental: My Truth is…

She took the trouble to tell me the truth.

Emotional: My emotions are…

Immensely grateful, compassion and love.

Physical: My physical sensations are…

Body feels still.

Physical Action: My actions are…

To thank her.

Spiritual: I am open to…

Feeling grateful to her.

STEP FOUR SELF Empowerment

Test the original thought believed to see what's changed.

Mental: The thought I believed at Step 1 was…

How dare you say I'm too busy.

Emotional: My emotions have changed to…

No emotional reaction, neutral.

Physical: My physical sensations have changed to…

Stillness.

Physical Action: My actions have changed to…

There is no action to take with this thought anymore as it is gone.

Spiritual: This statement is true for me. 'I am no longer closed to … I am open to… (life / the situation /

person).

I am no longer closed to her and my True Self, I am open to her and life.

Outcomes: To complete Step 4 we write out the outcomes to the situation.

Immediate Outcomes: (Internal Situation) Immediate Outcomes will be the change to your thoughts, emotions, physical sensations, actions, and being open.

I felt humbled and grateful to her for pointing out the truth, so my emotions and thoughts about her changed immediately, as well as my behaviour towards her.

Life Outcomes: (External Situation) Life Outcomes will be evident in the moment if the SEJ is done as the situation arises or appear later if the process is done retrospectively.

I scheduled a meeting with the student to sort out her concerns. I now endeavour to listen to the students about what their issues/concerns are instead of chastising them for interrupting me, as well as replying to their emails to acknowledge that I have received their correspondence.

Worksheet 3

CAREER EXAMPLE – A client that believed he wasn't good enough.

The following worksheet was completed by a Sales Consultant working in Cyber Security. He was new at his job, although he had worked in the industry for over 20 years. He had been asked to give a presentation. A month went by where he ignored every request to complete the presentation. Quite simply he suffered mentally, emotionally, and physically until the day he did the SEJ. His thoughts tortured him, he was emotionally drained ashamed and scared, he carried stress in his body and was completely closed. It was affecting his personal relationships and his work.

STEP ONE: Self Awareness

Situation...
Recall a situation that caused you to suffer, maybe you felt distressed, hurt, angry, sad, disappointed, or upset. Once you have this situation note it here:

I have been told that I need to record a 25-minute presentation on a new product that we sell, that is going to be seen and marked by VP's in the US. I only joined the company 2 months ago. I have been ignoring this email for a month and the VP in the US has just emailed me to say that I'm the only person who hasn't recorded a video presentation.

The Story…

Write here the 'story' your mind is telling about the situation. It is important you do not censor your thoughts, write them exactly as they appear to you, no matter how dark, petty, unkind, or judgmental they are.

Oh my god how am I expected to do this as I've only just joined the company, oh no what am I going to do? I can't do this as I don't know anything about this, and I'm trying to learn the product that I'm working on now. I can't do this; I don't know how, and everyone is going to know that I don't know what I'm talking about – what do I do?

I can't believe they expect me to do this as I'm new. Everyone will know that I don't know what I'm doing, and I don't have the time to learn this new stuff before I present. I'm not good enough to do this.

I cannot believe they are asking me to do

this, this is ridiculous!

List your thoughts...

Once the story has been written list the thoughts that grab your attention.

1. I can't do this.

2. I don't know how.

3. I don't know what I'm talking about.

4. I don't know what I'm doing.

5. I don't have the time.

6. I'm not good enough.

From the above list extract just one thought you would like to work on and put that thought through the 4 bodies.

Mental: The thought I believe is...

I can't do this.

Emotional: The emotions I experience when I believe this thought are...

Ashamed, scared.

Physical: When I believe this thought my bodily sensations are...

My body is slumped and tight.

Physical Action: When I believe this thought my actions are…

Ignore the email.

Spiritual: When I believe this thought I am closed to…

I am closed to the task. I am closed to the truth.

STEP TWO SELF Regulation

Sit in Silence and greet the thought you believe. Remember as you sit with the thought you stop thinking, in other words you do not run with this thought or add new thoughts to it, you simply remain open, observing the thought with no judgment. In this open state a Truth will rise from within you.

Or…

Climb the ladder of Truth!

List some opposites until a thought resonates with you.

_____

_____

_____

_____

_____

Mental: My Truth is…

I can do this.

Emotional: The emotions I experience when I allow space for this Truth are…

Inspired, excited.

Physical: With this Truth my bodily sensations are…

Body is upright.

Physical Action: With this Truth my actions are…

To do the recorded presentation.

Spiritual: With this Truth I am open to…

I am open to the knowing that I can and will complete the task.

STEP THREE SELF Confidence

We are now at Step 3, and here you quite simply look for
evidence and mirrors to support your new Truth. These
must again rise from within you, they MUST NOT come
from mind. Simply sit and allow this to happen. A good
starting point is to add the word 'because' at the end of
the new realised Truth. Remember 'mirrors' are thoughts
we project onto others, and so we need to claim them
back for ourselves. Mirrors tend to show themselves as
you go deeply into the evidence.

Write your evidence and highlight your mirrors here:

I can do this because I'm a really good
presenter and all I need to do is a bit of
training on the product and then I can put
together a really great presentation.

I can present, I can learn, I've been in IT
for 20 years so I do know my stuff, so I am
going to use this presentation as a great
opportunity to show what I CAN do!

I have presented literally 100's of times to
customers and colleagues, and I'm a fast
learner. All I need to do is take some time
to prepare, practice, and I can do a great
presentation.

I realise that it is a truth I am new
however this does not stop me from
presenting and doing a good job, to the

best of my ability, as I do know how to present, I can research the product. I was using the thought "I am new' to justify not taking any action!

Mirror

I was judging with my thought 'I cannot believe they are asking me to do this, this is ridiculous!'

I can't believe I'm asking myself to do this, this is ridiculous. It is ridiculous the pressure I am placing upon myself, not them, me! They are simply asking me to do my job. I am the one putting the pressure on. It's part of my job and this task isn't anything out of the ordinary. They are simply asking me to learn a new product, understand it, and be able to present it as if I was presenting it to a customer.

Once again, we go through the 4 bodies. This time choose either a Truth from Step 3 or if the most empowering Truth is still the one at Step 2 you can use this one again.

Mental: My Truth is...

I can do this!

Emotional: My emotions are…

Excited, inspired, joy.

Physical: My physical sensations are…

Very upright.

Physical Action: My actions are…

Record the presentation.

Spiritual: I am open to…

I am open to recording the presentation.

STEP FOUR SELF Empowerment

Test the original thought believed to see what's changed.

Mental: The thought I believed at Step 1 was…

I can't do this.

Emotional: My emotions have changed to…

Neutral.

Physical: My physical sensations have changed to…

Feel normal, very upright.

Physical Action: My actions have changed to...

Nothing to do.

Spiritual: This statement is true for me. 'I am no longer closed to... I am open to... (life / the situation / person).

I am no longer closed to doing the recording, I am open to recording the presentation, and the truth that I can and will.

Outcomes: To complete Step 4 we write out the outcomes to the situation.

Immediate Outcomes: (Internal Situation) Immediate Outcomes will be the change to your thoughts, emotions, physical sensations, actions, and being open.

The outcome was – I am excited to do the task. I feel excited and empowered.

Life Outcomes: (External Situation) Life Outcomes will be evident in the moment if the SEJ is done as the situation arises or appear later if the process is done retrospectively.

I did about 20 minutes of study on the new product, recorded the 25-minute video in one take.

A few days later:

I came joint 1st in the WORLD! Out of just under 100 people who did this presentation globally, I came joint 1st. The other 2 people who I drew with had all been with the company a long time and I came above everyone else in the European team. I went from a place of not doing the presentation to coming joint 1st!

Can you see how this client could have easily continued to suffer, maybe even been reprimanded if he had not done the presentation. And look how much he did suffer until he did the SEJ.

Isn't it interesting (and disturbing) how much we let ourselves suffer before we will do something to end the suffering? We simply believe thoughts that justify our suffering.

How long do you suffer for before you bring back joy?

Many people suffer because they believe their 'stories' and so never question them. BUT, if you are suffering mentally and emotionally question those thoughts, even the one that says, 'This thought doesn't need questioning.' The thoughts you believe the most, are definitely up for questioning, indeed EVERY thought is up for questioning.

Chapter Twenty-three

Einstein and the SEJ

At Step 2, 3 and 4 of the SEJ Process we ask you to swim in the 'silence' that Einstein refers to in this quote:

> *"I think 99 times and find nothing.*
> *I stop thinking, swim in silence and*
> *the Truth comes to me."*

Let us carefully look at another of his quotes.

> *"We cannot solve our problems with the same thinking*
> *we used when we created them."*

I was not aware of Einstein's quotes until a colleague introduced them to me. I was so inspired as they absolutely help to explain aspects of the SEJ Process perfectly. So, I will share with you why both quotes explain the spiritual dimension of the SEJ Process. Often a sticking point for some as the 'spiritual' is either unknown, or considered too 'airy fairy,' however the spiritual dimension (Truth) is the key element of the SEJ Process that brings the peace, joy, freedom, and resolution that the individual is seeking. Let us look deeper at what Einstein had to say about it.

At Step 1 of the SEJ we naturally look at the problem, this being the only step of the Process where we do so. The problem as seen comes from the false self. The remaining 3 steps are solution focused, (it is a solution focused process), through these steps we work from the True Self. Therefore, we do not use the same thinking to solve the problem as was used to create it, indeed we do not use any thinking at all!

All thoughts about the problem are written at Step 1. And at Step 2 we begin to action Einstein's words, and *'swim in silence'*, where thinking has no place.

When a person is unaware of the spiritual aspect, they will endeavour to think through a problem only to find the solution is elusive. Thinking merely serves in the continuous churning over of the problem in their mind. Therefore, although a person genuinely thinks they are solution focused, that they are using mind to find the answers, only ever will this serve to bring the individual back to the problem, or to inevitably bring a solution that is memory-based so repetitive in nature, anchored in the past. Anything that repeats prevents an individual from realising their full potential, as the True Self, where potential is limitless.

At Step 2 we ask you to 'sit' with the original thought believed or 'make friends' with the thought. Here it is a request to be still, observing the thought believed, this is the same as to *swim in silence*. However, a person will frequently initially find they are struggling with simply sitting and allowing a space for the thought to communicate with them. They find it difficult to be open to the thought and not push it away with more unconscious thoughts, as mind loves to add to the 'story' recorded at Step 1.

When Einstein says we need to stop thinking, he is not necessarily saying we must stop all thoughts, as this will be impossible in the initial stages. No, you simply need to let thoughts pass without giving them your attention or adding new thoughts.

Typically sitting in silence takes practice, you can call this meditation, to simply sit and be still. As you master this, you will become a walking meditation. The profound stillness or silence is something that you then find is at the fore as the busy mind takes its proper place in the workings of the mechanics of your being (the four bodies). Because you are no longer identified with your mind it becomes more silent simply storing and accessing information as required. The result is a mind no longer relevant where the True Self speaks. This, in turn, brings the mind to ease.

"I think 99 times and find nothing I stop thinking, swim in silence, and the truth comes to me."

We can see that the continual thinking *'99 times'* with no real solution found is why we have Step 2 as the beginning of our solution. You will find this solution is called throughout the Process 'Truth', and the thinking is referred to as that which is 'false'.

As it takes practice to sit in the silence of Truth, we offer a 'climbing of the ladder' in which you 'climb the ladder of truth'. Anyone can do this as it requires only that you understand opposites. Therefore, a young child can easily do the SEJ Process.

At Step 3 of the SEJ Process we go deeper into the Truth that is realised and seen from a different level of consciousness. As a person works Step 3, they go deeper and deeper into Truth, it is both enlightening and freeing. When practicing the SEJ a person invariably finds they no longer need situations to change in their life to be happy, joyous, or peaceful, that all of this comes from within the moment they realise the 'Truth'.

Finally, at Step 4 we simply test the original thought believed. This will show there is no longer any truth for the individual in the original thought, as there is no emotional pull or physical body reactions. Freedom and joy are once more experienced as the natural state of being where suffering was once experienced, a deeper connection to the 'Truth' is established.

Chapter Twenty-four

What thoughts should I question?

Every thought should be questioned because you are quite simply not a fair judge of whether a thought is truthful or not (even though you may believe you are). Indeed, once you begin to practice the SEJ, you will be surprised to see how many of your thoughts are untruthful.

As you learn the SEJ, you will be guided towards the understanding of the truthful part your emotions play in your life, and if you think you already know, maybe question that thought. For many people don't truly understand the role of their emotions. Without exception you are not your emotions; they are a needed guide as to how connected or disconnected you are to Truth (your True Self).

It is challenging to properly monitor every thought we have, what is easier, is to notice how we are feeling. From this point we can trace back to the thought we believe that inevitably causes us to feel the way we do.

Let us look at some common thoughts people believe about themselves, and others:

'My husband/wife/partner doesn't listen to me.'
'People should be kinder than they are.'
'I am too fat/old/boring.'
'No-one loves me.'
'Children today are disrespectful.'

Such unconscious thoughts, of course, would cause us to feel, upset, hurt, anxious, maybe even depressed.

The list of common limiting thoughts believed is endless, repetitive, and stressful. Indeed, all the emotional stress we experience is due to unconscious thoughts we believe that are not based in reality. If there were no limiting thoughts, there would be no stress. Stress, therefore, is a reliable guide informing you that you are listening to a lie of the mind (false self).

People who are only just learning the SEJ often go to great lengths to justify their thoughts, to typically try and get me to understand why their personal thoughts are true and how their situation is different, this is the result of an unconscious mind. Once consciousness comes into the situation through the SEJ, people are suddenly able to see how they are justifying their right to be miserable and suffer.

I ask you what good reason is there ever to suffer your thoughts?

People confuse the situation that is appearing in their life with the thoughts they have about the situation, this is the fundamental reason they justify. Let us be clear here, I am not saying the personal situation is not happening, if you've lost your job, you've lost your job, which is what has happened. What I am saying is it's your thoughts about the situation that undoubtedly causes you to experience stress, for losing your job causes no emotional stress on its own, please consider this. Only your thoughts about the loss of your job causes stress. Once you believe those stressful thoughts, you suffer mentally, emotionally, and physically, and any action you then take will come from a place of fear and suffering will continue.

The fundamental question is do you value yourself enough to put an end to suffering, or is it more important to you that you are right? Now of course, even this compelling need to be 'right' comes from a thought believed, because if we were wrong, we might feel 'not good enough.' So, you see all thoughts once questioned will naturally take you to core thoughts that keep you trapped in a limited version of yourself.

Your very nature is limitless. The SEJ Process will awaken you to this limitless SELF and the more you question every thought the more your life will change for the better. People will notice how much more empowered you are. You will naturally see that fear no longer holds you back, life will once again be exciting and you'll be open to everything, just as you were when you were a child.

For many the joy of life has been lost, but not forever, you can be joyful again, you can experience the excitement that life once held for you. And if you hear your mind, say something like 'not me I'm too old,' or 'I'm stuck in my ways,' pick up an SEJ Worksheet and question those thoughts.

You are not 'too old' you are not 'stuck in your ways' because you are not your thoughts. The SEJ Process will enable you to lose all identification with your mind, emotions, and body, and re-introduce you to who you really are.

People typically ask why they cannot question their own thoughts, why do they need the SEJ. It's an understandable question. My answer is simple, without an enlightened process like the SEJ the questioner will inevitably go back into mind for their answers, none of which will come from a place of Truth.

Even if you are a person that has accessed this deeper dimension, until you experience a fundamental shift in consciousness, which enables you to both access the answers from within, and see reality exactly as it is, you will still fall victim to your unconscious thoughts and beliefs. It is therefore best for you to use an enlightened process that will enable you to experience a shift in consciousness that is ever present.

In addition, the Process supports in breaking the habit of mind, the steadfast belief that mind has your answers. You are not to blame for this error. Your mind has simply been conditioned as our educational and societal systems are based upon the belief in a 'mind' that provides your answers. It confuses intellect with knowledge, and the belief that you are your mind, emotions, and body.

Ultimately, the SEJ Process will enable the functioning of the mind to be re-introduced into regaining its proper place in the 'mechanics of your being.' This is discussed further in the SEJ training.

The question, 'why should I question my thoughts?' is often asked by new students of the SEJ, and rightfully so. My answer to this is, if you genuinely want to be able to manage yourself whatever life throws your way, be stress free, discover a passion for life, to live joyfully and reach your full potential why would you not give yourself the gift of questioning your thoughts?

I would add to this, do not wait until life gets too difficult, although of course you can begin there. Why not start right now? So that when life naturally brings you loss in whatever form: job, loved one, health... you are already equipped to manage, and more than manage, to stand fearless and full of passion for life.

Chapter Twenty-five

Your SELF Empowerment Journey

By using the SEJ, you begin to breakdown the identification with mind, the belief in a 'you' that is separate from everyone and life itself into the realisation of unity, that we are all one. Not only are you whole, but you are everything.

Now, whether you have been looking for Self Realisation, asking the question 'Who Am I?' Or you simply wish to be free of your suffering, to be happy. Whatever your reasons the SEJ will work for you, because the first step of the SEJ is to bring awareness to your limiting beliefs that cause you to suffer and experience a lesser or limited version of yourself.

As you continue your Self Empowerment Journey you will ultimately become Self Realised if this is your wish and desire. Does this happen overnight? Well, it can but for many the belief in a self that is false is so deeply embedded that it could take time. For your entire life, you've lived as this 'false self'. Only now are you being introduced to the 'True Self', be patient, become disciplined in your practice of the SEJ and watch the miracles happen.

It is for this reason that although I am happy to share with you the process, and indeed you can begin to use it straight away, it is highly advisable that you attend the SEJ Training and Practice Workshops to understand the teachings of the SEJ, why and how it works, and how it will work for you. Otherwise, you may misinterpret the worksheet; its application and the absolute power of the SEJ Process.

WARNING: Do not confuse the simplicity of the SEJ Process with its power and limitless potential.

The power of the SEJ will unfold within you and your life as you commit to using the process. It is not for the fainthearted. It is for those ready to transform themselves and consequently their lives.

We have proven that the SEJ works 100% of the time. Therefore, it will work for you 100% of the time as long as you do the process correctly. At Step 4 of the SEJ process if you have not become Self Realised in relation to the belief you are working on, you can access support through the various SEJ support services to find the corrections. Research data from Kingston University, demonstrating the success of the SEJ, can be found on the website.

Over time I realised how important it was to provide ongoing support to people because the journey of empowerment never ends, this is because your potential is truly limitless both in life and death. Look at those enlightened beings who have gone before us and the miracles they have performed. Is it wrong to compare yourself to such beings? NO, absolutely not.

Jesus said, "...*these and greater works than these shall ye do*...2. John 14:12. The full version of this quote also refers to beliefs and the importance of beliefs influencing our experience of life and self, although this quote has been misinterpreted over the years. It, of course, also refers to our limitless potential. We truly are limitless beings, limited only by an identification with a 'false self'.

As you begin and continue your Self Empowerment Journey, we at, the SEJ are here to guide and support however far you wish to go.

Chapter Twenty-six

The SEJ and the law of attraction

During a training event I used the example of Jesus and how he said we could all do 'greater works', being truly were limitless. This led into a discussion about the law of attraction and the SEJ process. I shared that everyone could manifest fish as Jesus did in the feeding of the 5000. It's just that the manifestation appears in a different way. I continued that if they wanted to manifest a fish right now, they would get into their car, drive to the supermarket, make the purchase, and return with a fish. What a powerful manifestation!

This is not like Jesus was the consensus.

You see, when I say we are all limitless I mean limitless, it is not just a fanciful idea, and equally Jesus was not lying when he said, 'greater works than these shall ye do.' We simply have thoughts in place that we believe which prevent us from manifesting the fish as Jesus did. Just notice within yourself any resistance. What are the thoughts? 'It's impossible', 'it's blasphemy', 'I'm not Jesus.'

If we can manifest the car and the supermarket that leads

to the fish, then we can manifest. So, why not dissolve the beliefs about the car and supermarket as necessary to the manifestation and go straight to manifesting the fish? Again, because you don't believe you can. Yet this is what the SEJ process does, it dissolves the beliefs that prevent you from realising the SELF. A Self that is limitless.

I would like to share with you an example of how I was able to manifest beyond my limiting beliefs.

One day it came to me to move house, just like that, time to move. I had not been thinking about moving; I had a house with a mortgage that my husband, daughter, and I lived in. Hence, moving was not going to happen quickly, according to my mind. Still, I woke one morning and absolutely knew it was time to relocate. I was inspired to look on the internet immediately to find a new home in the countryside away from the city. I discovered the perfect home, made the call, and viewed it within a day.

The agent commented on how quickly the property would go and that I was fortunate to be able to see it so soon after calling to view. On viewing the property, I asked if I could come straight to the office to sort out the paperwork. At the same time, I was aware of thoughts in my mind attempting to get my attention. Thoughts such as 'how will I pay for it, I have the mortgage to pay, I can't afford rent as well.' Now this was an absolute truth, I couldn't afford to pay for two homes, and yet I knew this was right for me, so the rest, the finer details until shown to me, were none of my business. At the agent's office, they asked for my financial information, so they could ensure I could pay. Of course, I knew they would not meet the requirements, and these words just fell out of my mouth. 'Can I pay for 6 months' rent in advance?' Well, my mind had a field day with this, 'Six months' rent up front, where was that amount of money coming from?' Again, I ignored my mind and continued. The agent said she had never had a request like this before and would have to phone the owners, she did, they said yes and all I had to do was pay a small amount to secure the rental property.

On my return home I informed my husband I had secured the house, now I just needed the 6 months' rent to appear! And it did, in the form of a tax rebate.

I could give you many examples like this, not all of them around money, but money is often a sign of freedom from suffering for so many. True freedom from suffering comes when we realise Truth, and in so doing whatever is needed in terms of manifestations will just come.

The law of attraction is indeed a powerful law, yet many don't manifest what they desire, and this is for one reason only. As given previously you have beliefs preventing the ultimate manifestation. And for many what they think they want to manifest only perpetuates a limited version of themselves (false self). When you access Truth, all that is needed will come. It will be beyond your wildest dreams because it will be the manifestation of all that is your absolute Truth, beyond anything your mind can imagine.

Chapter Twenty-seven

Try it for yourself

When sharing with an audience how to do the SEJ Process and discussing whether it works, I invariably say:

'Don't believe me; I don't want you to, the Process speaks for itself. It didn't come from me it arose from within me, it came from Truth, and as you and I are inseparably connected by Truth the Process was never mine to keep, it has always been yours and now you are ready to receive it.

Therefore, attempt it for yourself, do the Process and change your world.'

Pointers:

The Process works 100% of the time. If it does not work for you, it will only be because you are unpractised in achieving silence and allowing Truth to speak. Put differently, you will have gone back into mind for your answers. So, support is on offer via our SEJ Practice Workshops. These are online webinars in which you get to:

1. Ask questions about the SEJ Process.
2. Obtain practice corrections.

3. Bring along your SEJ Worksheets for analysis, questions, discussion or sharing.

4. Develop your 'Sitting in Silence' practice.

Chapter Twenty-eight

Frequently Asked Questions

How can you have positive thoughts when you can't always control what happens around you?

As you use the Process, you will find that life is working for you not against you, then the need to control what happens around you will go. This does not mean that you will not take positive action, but any action you do take will be based on Truth not a positive thought.

Is it bad to show your emotions? How can I control them?

Emotions are simply your beliefs finding expression, and therefore aid as a barometer showing you how connected or disconnected you are from Truth. Whether you show them or not is irrelevant in terms of your SEJ, what is important is that you notice your emotions, once you take more notice of them and practice the Process there will be no concerns about when or how to express them, and any need to control them will fall away as you see their purpose and value as a barometer.

I try to not think negatively but the thoughts won't stop. How do I stop them?

I understand that a busy mind can be very overwhelming, yet your mind is busy only because you have not let go of those thoughts that no longer serve you. This is because you have not known how to, or even which thoughts to let go of, this is what the SEJ will do for you.

Next time your mind is busy liken it to a bin that is full, you would not keep putting more stuff into the bin without first emptying it, and yet more is added to the mind until you can no longer cope. Empty your mind by putting the thoughts through the SEJ and you will become still and joyful again.

What if after completing the Process I still feel the same, does this mean it doesn't work for everyone?

The Process works 100% of the time if you do it correctly and stick to the Process. The most common mistake is in relation to allowing space for the Truth to rise from within, it can take practice. Sometimes in the beginning stages people go back into their mind for answers, and this never works, be gentle with yourself and persevere, it will work for you.

Can the SEJ be applied to any situation in life?

Yes. This is the beauty of it.

You see the situation is never the problem, it is only ever your thoughts about the situation that are the problem. You may not have the power to change the situation, but you can change how you think, and therefore feel and act in relation to the situation.

How can I deal with people around me that are suffering with their mental health?

By addressing your own thoughts about them. Once you can come back into a place of Truth, how you deal with them will change in relation to how you now think about them.

Isn't it normal to have negative thoughts?

It is normal to have thoughts, whether you perceive them as positive or negative is a different matter and down to your own personal programming. Thoughts are not personal they are simply memory triggered through stimuli. The question is, does the thought cause you to suffer? If it does why suffer, do the SEJ.

You have said life is on our side, how can this be so when there are such terrible things that happen?

I know this may be difficult for the mind to grasp because its experience is one of separation. When you practice the SEJ at some point you will begin to experience this for yourself and that is what's important here, that this becomes your experience. Otherwise, it is like me sharing with you what honey tastes like, until you taste it the mind can only guess.

Are you saying we should just accept when terrible things happen?

I am not saying you should or should not accept them, only you will know what to do with any given situations as you question your thoughts about them. The SEJ is not a passive tool, indeed it is based upon changing your actions so that you are able to respond to life rather than react, when you react nothing changes.

If we are to create a different experience, we must first look to change the experience within ourselves, this in turn will alter our external experience, allowing us to act according to our personal Truth which is always loving and inclusive.

Does the SEJ Process build off any religious Processes e.g., Buddhism, Taoism?

There was a period of time when SEJ students would ask me if I had heard of various spiritual teachers and processes, because they saw something in the SEJ that was in these too.

The assumption was often (not always), that the SEJ had been developed based upon these spiritual teachings. Of course, it was not, I knew nothing about spirituality when I woke up to Truth. I truly would not even call the SEJ spiritual, but I understand the need to give labels, for me it is simply about seeing Truth. I simply woke up to Truth and from that moment on people were drawn to me, they wanted to know what I knew, and it has continued to this day.

The mind seems to find it difficult to comprehend that an ordinary person can just 'wake up', but this is just what happened. I am not well educated, I have no spiritual background, I am just like you, and therefore what happened to me can happen to you too. Isn't this beautiful to know?

A number of years after writing the SEJ I was inspired to look at various spiritual texts, both old and new. I saw that the texts were indeed the same Truth given in the SEJ Process, because there is only one Truth. What I also saw was that the SEJ was a tool for everyone to realise this powerful Truth for themselves, the texts gave teachings, but seldom did they give a tool within which to realise the Self.

How do I get over my past?

By questioning the thoughts about the past that arise within you in the present. I would start with the thought 'How do I get over my past,' and I am not being flippant, try it, and see what happens.

You have said 'you are both the question and the answer,'

how is this so?

The question arises from within you as a thought yet to be questioned, an emotion felt and life experience yet to be looked at. As you do the Process you will find that in Truth only you have your answers in relation to all of these experiences which are unique to you.

What do you mean when you say 'no one and no-thing' can fix you?

I realised through my own experiences that I was looking for the 'one', that one person or thing whether doctor, therapist, consultant, tablet, treatment etc. (I tried most things) to fix me. Only when I woke up to Truth did I see that the 'one' I was looking for was me. I had my own answers, and although it felt daunting at first, it was also extremely liberating.

How does the SEJ compare to talking therapies?

It doesn't compare. It can't be compared because it is completely different. Generally, therapies require you to engage with another person, the therapist who discusses your past and future with you. They also ask that you use your mind to address thoughts, emotions, and behaviours, and look for reasons as to why you feel the way you do.

The SEJ requires that you engage only with your True SELF, there is no therapist as one is not needed, you don't look outside of yourself for a reason for your situation, you look inside, and there is no discussion about the past only an awareness of how the past is affecting your present.

When going through depression I realised that as kind and caring as my therapists were, and extremely knowledgeable in their field, they too only knew what they had learnt, and so it was limited, Truth is unlimited. Only you can access Truth and the SEJ shows you how.

The SEJ works with the mind, body, and emotions, therefore isn't it just like Cognitive Behavioural Therapy?

As with CBT we agree that thoughts and beliefs, can affect a person's feelings and behaviours. Finding resolution does not come from this awareness, it comes from Truth. This isn't found in CBT.

Einstein said:

"I think 99 times and find nothing. I stop thinking, swim in silence, and the truth comes to me."

We are only interested in Truth, the SEJ Process will enable you to question your thoughts and swim in the silence, then Truth will come to you. Only Truth has the power to dissolve your thoughts and limiting beliefs, to such an extent that you can be free of suffering, reach your full potential, and know who you truly are beyond thought.

CBT limits you to what you can imagine and derive through investigating thought. Whereas CBT looks towards the mind to find solutions to your negative thoughts and behaviours, the SEJ doesn't look at all to the mind for the answers, not at all, answers can never be found in the mind because the mind can only give you what it already knows.

Challenging thoughts, which CBT does is only the beginning. The SEJ is about giving you what you don't know beyond mind, so that you can change your life forever, reach your full potential and really experience freedom from suffering. How? The SEJ is a solution focused process that separates you from thought, rather than reinforcing thought, it enables you to live as your True Self, rather than a false self which is based upon identification with thought.

If the SEJ doesn't involve thinking to address problems what exactly is happening?

You are going beyond thought.

Remember all your thoughts are 'old news' as they come from memory, they simply appear new because the life situation (what we call stimuli in the Process) is new, and so the memory-based thought triggered by the life situation appears new too, but it is not. So, you repeat patterns of behaviour and thought, it is a never-ending cycle that limits you. Therefore, the SEJ Process does two things:

1. It dissolves the memory-based thoughts which limit you.

2. You learn to go beyond thought for answers and ultimately become Self-realised, living as your True Limitless SELF.

My thoughts just don't stop, how can I stop them?

I used to live in a world of continuous thought too, my mind was always busy, and I felt overwhelmed and anxious most of the time. I could not turn my thoughts off (except if I had a drink or watched TV). I would never have believed I would be where I am today. If stopping the busy mind is your goal just do the SEJ.

When you do the SEJ Process, you will see that thoughts will lose their power over you. As a distance is created between you and your thoughts, they will simply fall away from you. There is no trying to stop thought, this never works, only self-enquiry works.

The SEJ is about questioning your thoughts so that they dissolve. As you dissolve thought you begin to separate yourself from mind, and go deeper into the True Self, realising that YOU are NOT your thoughts.

Chapter Twenty-nine

Conclusion

It is time for you to continue your Self Empowerment Journey.

Practice is essential for you to master the process, initially you may need some support and practical guidance, and my team and I are here to support you in the following ways:

1. To ensure you are doing the Process correctly and that you properly understand the practices and principles you can attend the SEJ Process training event.

2. For ongoing support with your practice and to ask questions you can attend the weekly SEJ Practice Workshops.

For more information go to our website:

www.thesej.co.uk
www.jacquelinemaryphillips.com

Appendix

On the following pages you will discover resources to support you in completing the SEJ Worksheet.

i.   **Emotional Barometer:** Sometimes it is difficult to pinpoint exactly what we are feeling, this scale although not exhaustive, will support in guiding you through your emotions. It also enables you to see the journey between the lower emotions experienced when we believe thoughts that limit us, and the higher emotions experienced when Truth is realised.

ii. **Physical Sensations:** When we are not used to paying attention to the body it can be difficult to articulate exactly what the bodily sensations are. This list will provide some known sensations, you can add others using your own words.

iii. **Collective Beliefs**: A list of collective thoughts believed when in the unconscious state. It is not an exhaustive list; it does however give you awareness of the type of thoughts that can lead to stress and psychological suffering. These thoughts are common in the collective consciousness of humankind.

iv. **The SEJ Worksheet**: A template of the SEJ Worksheet for you to use. You can also access the worksheets via the website.

Vibrational Emotional Barometer

Love   Joy   Passion Freedom   Euphoria   Bliss   Empowered
Happiness   Gratitude   Compassion Inspired
Confidence Open-Hearted   Serene
Worthy   Eagerness At Ease   Light-Hearted
Hopefulness   Acceptance Encouraged
Neutral point – Silence
Doubtful   Insecurity   Lonely Rejection   Disappointment
Worry   Pessimism   Frustration Impatience   Irritation
Anger   Rage Hatred   Fear
Sadness   Abandoned   Ashamed Anxiety   Unloved
Despair   Disempowerment   Grief Depression   Hopelessness

Physical Sensations

Aglow, Achy, Alive, Airy

Bruised, Blocked, Brittle, Bubbly, Burning, Buzzy, Breathless

Cosy, Calm, Closed, Congested, Cool, Cold, Clammy, Clenched, Constricted, Constrained

Damp, Dark, Disappearing, Disconnected, Dense, Dizzy, Dull, Drained, Deflated, Dry throat

Empty, Electric, Energised, Expanding, Expansive

Fluid, Flowing, Floating, Fiery, Frantic, Frozen, Full, Fluttery, Faint, Frail, Fragile, Fuzzy

Gurgling

Hard, Heavy, Hot, Hollow

Imploding, Icy, Intense, Inflated, Itchy

Jagged, Jumbly, Jittery, Jumpy

Knotted

Light, Loose

Moving, Moved, Melting

Nervy, Nauseous, Numb

Open

Who Am I?

Paralysed, Pounding, Pressure, Prickly, Pulled, Pulsating, Puffy, Pit in the stomach

Quirky, Quaking, Quiet, Quivering, Queasy

Radiating, Ragged, Raw, Restless, Relaxed, Releasing, Rigid, Red Hot,

Stretchy, Small, Spacious, Smooth, Shaky, Sore, Streaming Sharp, Shivery, Soft, Spinning, Sticky, Still, Strong, Sweaty, Spacey, Suffocating, Soft, Stiff, Sparkly, Slouched, Sensitive, Searing

Tender, Tense, Thick, Throbbing, Tight, Tingling, Trembley, Tickly, Twitchy, Tired

Wakeful, Warm, Wobbly, Wooden

Collective Beliefs

Examples of unconscious thoughts	
• I need to make a decision	• I don't want to look like a fool
• I can't do anything right	• I need a partner to be happy
• I am responsible for upsetting others	• I need a job to be happy
• There's too much to do	• I need money to be happy
• I don't have enough time	• They rejected me
• I need to understand	• They don't trust me
• I need to get it right	• I can't trust myself
• I can't get it wrong	• They think they know me
• I should know what to do	• People should not lie
• I don't know what to do	• People should show more respect
• I'm not good enough	• I know what I need to do, what is best
• I am a failure	• I am right

Who Am I?

• I missed my chance	• Something bad is going to happen
• It is too late	• I should be different
• They should know better	• I'm too fat
• They should listen to me	• I am too thin
• I know what is best for others	• It is my fault
• I know I am right	• It is your fault
• I am worthless	• There's something wrong with me
• I have low self-esteem	• Women are too emotional
• Everyone is judging me	• The world is a bad place
• I know what they are thinking	• People are destroying the environment
• Life is difficult	• People are destroying our earth
• People should be grateful	• People are hurting our animals
• My boss / friends / family should appreciate me	• People should keep their promises

Who Am I?

• People cannot be trusted	• People will let you down
• They do not care about me	• My body should be healthy
• I have no money	• I am a spiritual person
• Life is not fair	• I must work hard to survive
• I did it wrong	• I need to be in control
• I do not belong	• They made me feel this way
• People should not be angry	• I have a 'life's purpose'
• People should be more loving	• I need to know my life's purpose
• I'm no good	• I feel sad
• I am a total failure	• Nothing ever goes my way
Add your own thoughts.	•
•	•
•	•
•	•
•	•
•	•

SEJ Worksheet

STEP ONE: Self Awareness

Situation...

Recall a situation that caused you to suffer, maybe you felt distressed, hurt, angry, sad, disappointed, or upset. Once you have this situation note it here:

The Story...

Write here the 'story' your mind is telling about the situation. It is important you do not censor your thoughts, write them exactly as they appear to you, no matter how dark, petty, unkind, or judgmental they are.

List your thoughts...

Once the story has been written list the thoughts that grab your attention.

1.

2.

3.

4.

5.

6.

From the above list extract just one thought you would like to work on and put that thought through the 4 bodies.

Mental: The thought I believe is...

Emotional: The emotions I experience when I believe this thought are...

Physical: When I believe this thought my bodily sensations are...

Physical Action: When I believe this thought my actions are...

Spiritual: When I believe this thought I am closed to…

STEP TWO SELF Regulation

Sit in Silence and greet the thought you believe. Remember as you sit with the thought you stop thinking, in other words you don't run with this thought or add new thoughts to it, you simply remain open, observing the thought with no judgment. In this open state a Truth will rise from within you.

Or…

Climb the ladder of Truth!

List some opposites until a thought resonates with you.

_____

_____

_____

_____

_____

Mental: My Truth is…

Emotional: The emotions I experience when I allow space for this Truth are…

Physical: With this Truth my bodily sensations are…

Physical Action: With this Truth my actions are…

Spiritual: With this Truth I am open to…

STEP THREE SELF Confidence

We are now at Step 3, and here you quite simply look for **evidence and mirrors** to support your new Truth. These must again rise from within you, they MUST NOT come from mind. Simply sit and allow this to happen. A good starting point is to add the word 'because' at the end of the new realised Truth. Remember 'mirrors' are thoughts we project onto others, and so we need to claim them back for ourselves. Mirrors tend to show themselves as you go deeply into the evidence.

Write your evidence and highlight your mirrors here:

Once again, we go through the 4 bodies. This time choose either a Truth from Step 3 or if the most empowering Truth is still the one at Step 2 you can use this one again.

Mental: My Truth is…

Emotional: My emotions are…

Physical: My physical sensations are…

Physical Action: My actions are…

Spiritual: I am open to…

STEP FOUR SELF Empowerment

Test the original thought believed to see what's changed.

Mental: The thought I believed at Step 1 was…

Emotional: My emotions have changed to…

Physical: My physical sensations have changed to…

Physical Action: My actions have changed to…

Spiritual: This statement is true for me. 'I am no longer closed to… I am open to… (life / the situation / person).

Outcomes: To complete Step 4 we write out the outcomes to the situation.

Immediate Outcomes:(Internal Experience) Immediate Outcomes are the changes to your thoughts, emotions, physical sensations, actions, and being open.

Life Outcomes: (External Experience) Life Outcomes will be evident in the moment if the SEJ is done as the situation arises or appear later if the process is done reflectively.

About the Author

When I was about 7 years old, I was asked what I was going to do when I grew up. I recall my answer very clearly even to this day, because even at that incredibly young age I was speaking from Truth. I remember being extremely curious as to the words that came out of my mouth wondering what on earth they meant. I replied to the question with *"I am going to be a teacher, but not like one of those at school."*

Well, although I did not understand what I was saying at the time, since waking up to Truth, without any thought of making speaking of Truth into a career. I became a 'teacher.' An accidental teacher sought by those wanting to experience what I know, the rest as they say is history.

Printed in Great Britain
by Amazon

80275078R00092